AMERICANIZED

AMERICANIZED

Rebel Without a Green Card

SARA SAEDI

Alfred A. Knopf ⟶ New York

THIS IS A BORZOI BOOK PUBLISHED BY ALFRED A. KNOPF

Visit us on the Web! GetUnderlined.com

Educators and librarians, for a variety of teaching tools, visit us at
RHTeachersLibrarians.com

Library of Congress Cataloging-in-Publication Data
Names: Saedi, Sara, author.
Title: Americanized : rebel without a green card / Sara Saedi.
Description: First edition. | New York : Alfred A. Knopf, [2018] | Summary: In San
Jose, California, in the 1990s, teenaged Sara keeps a diary of life as an Iranian American
and her discovery that she and her family entered as undocumented immigrants.
Identifiers: LCCN 2017028259 (print) | LCCN 2016057751 (ebook) |
ISBN 978-1-5247-1779-7 (trade) | ISBN 978-1-5247-1780-3 (lib. bdg.) |
ISBN 978-1-5247-1781-0 (ebook)
Subjects: | CYAC: Iranian Americans—Fiction. | Family life—California—
Fiction. | Immigrants—Fiction. | Illegal aliens—Fiction. | California—History—
20th century—Fiction.
Classification: LCC PZ7.1.S237 (print) | LCC PZ7.1.S237 Ame 2018 (ebook) |
DDC [Fic]—dc23

The text of this book is set in 12-point Apollo.

Printed in the United States of America
February 2018
10 9 8 7 6 5 4 3 2 1

First Edition

For Samira and Kia,
family by birth, best friends by choice

Contents

Introduction

Puberty is the equivalent of guerrilla warfare on your body. Society commonly refers to it as the awkward phase, but I've always preferred to call it the "everything totally sucks and I hate my life" phase. I, for one, don't miss 1993. That was the year I naively thought my biggest problems were my underdeveloped breasts, the cystic acne that had built a small colony on my chin, and the sad fact that my prettier best friend and I had set our sights on the same guy. Would our friendship fall apart over a boy? Would I ever outgrow my training bra? Would my skin ever clear up? These were the dilemmas that kept me up at night. I thought there was no way my life could get worse.

But I was wrong.

What seemed like a mundane afternoon would go down in history as the day my world crumbled. My older sister, Samira, and I were hanging out in the kitchen, probably dining on our favorite light Entenmann's coffee cake. I worked on my homework while Samira pored over job applications for a dozen or so retail stores at the posh Valley Fair mall in our hometown of San Jose, California. Our parents owned a small luggage business about a forty-minute drive away, and they were never home before dinnertime. And so the task of watching over my younger brother and me fell to my sister. But I was cool with that, because in my opinion, an older sibling had two primary reasons for living:

1. Expose their younger siblings to the harsh realities of the world.
2. Protect their younger siblings from the harsh realities of the world.

This story covers number 1. I don't think my sister derived any pleasure from blowing my carefully crafted reality to pieces, but maybe she couldn't handle being alone in her teen angst. My parents told her things they thought I was still too young to know, but I was nearly thirteen and it was time I learned the truth about our family. It was time I learned the truth about myself. And it was her duty in life to be the one to break it to me.

"No one will ever hire me," my sister said, frustrated. "I'm never gonna get to make my own money."

I wanted to tell her that as long as she could keep her somewhat problematic attitude in check during a job interview, I didn't think she'd have a problem finding long-term employment.

"Sure you will," I reassured her. "You already have sales experience working at the luggage store."

"That's different. I worked for Mom and Dad. All the stores at the mall want a Social Security number," she vented.

At the time, I'd never heard of the term "Social Security number."

"So?" I asked.

"*So* I don't have one," she responded. "And neither do you."

Her response clarified nothing. Who cared if we didn't have Social Security numbers? We had a phone number and an address. What else did a person need to apply for a job?

"You're not getting it," Samira continued. "The government doesn't know we exist. We could get deported at any time."

I heard the words as they came out of her mouth, but my young mind didn't know how to process them. Deported? I had trouble reconciling the definition of the word with the fact that we'd been living in the Bay Area for ten years.

"Like, they could send us back to Iran?"

"Yes," she said.

"Even Kia?" I asked. My brother was almost five years old then. He was objectively adorable. Why would anyone ever want to deport him?

"No," she explained. "He was born here. He's a citizen."

That entitled brat! I glared at him, sitting in the next room eating Oreos and watching *Teenage Mutant Ninja Turtles*, blissfully unaware that his sisters might get shipped back to the Islamic Republic. My anxiety tripled when Samira explained that not having a green card or a Social Security number also meant we were breaking the law simply by living in the United States.

"We're *illegal aliens*."

This was before "undocumented immigrant" became the more commonly used (and politically correct) term. The words "illegal aliens" echoed through my head. Suddenly hormonal acne and microscopic boobs paled in comparison to the revelation that I was a criminal. And, apparently, an alien? How would I explain this to my law-abiding, human friends? They'd probably want nothing to do with me once they learned I technically wasn't allowed to be living in the country. If this got out, I could lose everything.

But when my parents came home that night, they assured me that no one was going to deport us. We weren't criminals or extraterrestrials. We were trying to get green cards. It would all work out and no one would have to go back to Iran.

"So we won't have to leave America?" I asked.

*"Na, Baba!"** my dad said to me. This sort of translates to "No way, Jose!"

But I wasn't exactly convinced. That night, when I went to bed, I was no longer worried about eighth-grade love triangles or whether it was possible that Clearasil was just an elab-

---

*The direct translation of the Farsi word *baba* is "dad." (You'll be seeing that word a lot when I refer to my dad.)

orate scam that gave insecure teens false hope. I was worried what my life would look like if I had to say good-bye to my friends and move back to Iran. My Farsi was rusty at best. Being forced to wear a head scarf would only accentuate my bad skin. I'd already been living in the United States for a decade. How would I ever adjust? My sister's warning stayed with me like a refrain through the rest of my teen years:

We. Could. Get. Deported. At. Any. Time.

There was only one appropriate reaction:

Holy. Shit.

Yes, my sin—my greater sin . . . and even my greatest sin is that I nationalized Iran's oil industry and discarded the system of political and economic exploitation by the world's greatest empire. This at the cost to myself, my family; and at the risk of losing my life, my honor, and my property. With God's blessing and the will of the people, I fought this savage and dreadful system of international espionage and colonialism.

—Mohammad Mossadegh, *former prime minister of Iran,
defending himself against charges of treason,
December 19, 1953*

Chapter One

◆ ★ ◆

A Brief (but Juicy) History
of My Birthplace (and My Birth)

I swear on my autographed copy of Ethan Hawke's debut novel that this chapter will not be dull, so please don't skim or skip over it. If you won't take my word for it and have no vested interest in broadening your worldview, here's the most important takeaway: Iran is not pronounced *i-RAN;* it's pronounced *e-RON.* Spread the word. Tell all your friends. Tweet it. Shout it from the rooftops. Correct people. It'll make you sound smart and cultured. On behalf of my fellow Iranians (*e-RON-ians*), we thank you.

Now for those juicy historical details you were promised! Real talk: Iran has dealt with its fair share of strife and political unrest. And while I'm not one to point fingers or lay blame . . . the United States and Britain were totally at fault. Okay, that's not entirely accurate. The West might not be directly accountable for all of Iran's drama, but they definitely stirred the pot back in the early 1950s. During that time, Prime Minister Mohammad Mossadegh ruled Iran. Personally, I consider the man a hero. He was a democratically elected leader, and a progressive. But his main claim to fame was that he nationalized Iran's oil industry. Prior to Mossadegh, the country's most valuable resource was under British control. But why let the Brits instead of Iranians profit off of Iran's most lucrative industry? That's the equivalent of Kanye West pocketing all the profits from *1989* (the Taylor Swift album, not the year in history). Thus, Iran told the British oil companies to hit the road, and the Brits were predictably pissed. Mossadegh to Britain: "Bye, Felicia."

So Britain decided to call in a favor from their bestie: the United States. If texting had existed at that time, then Winston Churchill would have sent President Eisenhower a bunch of crying-face emojis. According to Churchill, they needed to get rid of Mossadegh. The United States was initially reluctant to get involved, but Britain pointed out that Iran's beloved prime minister had newly gained the support of the Tudeh Party (an Iranian communist party) and the country would eventually go red. (Oh, hell no, it wouldn't. Our man Mossadegh wasn't even a fan of socialism. Not to mention, the Tudeh Party frequently turned against him.) So Eisenhower said, "We're in!" And that's when the CIA and Britain's Secret Intelligence Service decided to buddy up and formulate a secret coup to overthrow Mossadegh. They called it Operation Ajax. Possibly named for the mythological Greek hero or the cleaning product. Your guess is as good as mine. It was decided that Iran's ruling monarch at the time, Shah Mohammad Reza Pahlavi (yes, "Mohammad" is like the "Mike" of Iran), would take over for Mossadegh. Initially, the shah said, "You people are nuts! Everyone loves Mossadegh. You're asking me to commit political suicide." But then the United States threatened to dismiss the shah as well, and he was like: "How soon do we get this overthrow party started?"

Long story short, the coup was a success. Mossadegh was jailed for three years and then placed under house arrest, till his death in 1967. Kind of ironic that today the United States would really love more democratic countries in the Middle East, and Iran *was* one, until the CIA got involved. *J'accuse!* The short-term wins for the United States and United Kingdom included regaining limited access to Iran's oil by having a stake in a holding company called Iranian Oil Participants, or IOP. After the overthrow of Mossadegh, public opinion in Iran was so against the Brits taking total control of the country's oil supply again that IOP was the United Kingdom's next best option.

Meanwhile, post-coup, the shah and his family were living it up on diamond-studded thrones until everything went off the rails again in 1978. This time, the political unrest wasn't orchestrated by foreign powers. It was the people of Iran who were fed up with the monarchy, and they had good reason. For starters, the Pahlavi family was ridiculously rich, and shamelessly extravagant with their money. Iranians respected properly gained wealth, but they objected to the shah's fortune because much of it was stolen from the people. Which is why, beyond the walls of the palace, the country's economy was in the crapper. Families struggled to put food on the table, while the royal family spent hundreds of millions of dollars on parties to celebrate the monarchy. Not to mention that the shah had a secret police force called SAVAK, which had a reputation for torturing and executing anyone who opposed the monarchy. (Side note: America and Israel helped establish SAVAK. In fact, the CIA helped train the officers, which means they played a significant role in the torture and murder of thousands of shah detractors.) But at this point, even the United States was over the shah because . . . wait for it . . . he increased the price of oil. The overwhelming dislike for the Pahlavi dynasty gave birth to the Iranian Revolution, and by then my parents were also fed up with the regime's inhumane tactics. My baba, Ali, joined the protests, and eventually the shah was exiled.

Mostly everyone in Iran: "SWEET!"

But with every revolution comes the risk that the new regime might suck worse than the old one, and some felt that happened when the Ayatollah Khomeini (the guy with the long beard and turban—"imam" accessories that many now associate with stereotypes like terrorism) came into power. Keep in mind that the Tehran of my parents' generation (during the shah's reign) was a burgeoning metropolis with European sensibilities. My maman* walked the streets of her

---

*Maman means "mom" in Farsi.

neighborhood in itty-bitty miniskirts, with her long, wavy brown hair blowing freely in the wind.

During his bachelor days, my dad regularly had girlfriends he could take out in public. The consumption of alcohol was legal, and no one had to worry about the religious police arresting them for throwing a coed party. Tehran (the country's capital) was a vacation hot spot, and a travel destination for many Westerners. Also, just so we're clear—my parents didn't travel around town on a camel. If you want to picture Tehran in your head, don't conjure up images of Agrabah (the fictional city in *Aladdin*). Think New York City.

But when Khomeini came to power, he founded the *Islamic* Republic of Iran and introduced Islamic law* to the country. Suddenly there were strict dress codes for women that required them to cover up their hair, men and women (unless they were married) were mostly segregated, Western music and movies were banned, and alcohol became illegal. For some, Khomeini was a total buzzkill. Of course, the new laws thrilled the country's religious citizens, but my mostly secular family wasn't having it. My mom had great hair. It would have been a cardinal sin to cover up those luscious chestnut locks. That said, while the country was deprived of my mom's shampoo-commercial-quality tresses, there were also benefits to the Islamic Revolution. For instance, the

*Islamic law (also referred to as Sharia) is a set of moral laws that come from the Qur'an instead of legislation by the people. Some aspects of Islamic law are observed in Iran's legal system, but today the country mostly operates under civil law, ratified by the parliament.

literacy rate in Iran nearly tripled (up to 97 percent, higher than the United States'), because social conservatives were comfortable with sending their daughters to school, now that their classmates would also be wearing head scarves. One could argue that the revolution oppressed women, while others could argue it helped liberate them.

Meanwhile, the shah and his family, now in exile, were desperately looking for a country to take them in. President Carter reluctantly allowed them into the United States so the shah could receive surgery for non-Hodgkin's lymphoma, but then all hell broke loose in Tehran. Iranians wanted the shah returned to the country so he could be tried for war crimes. When the United States refused to send him back, a bunch of Iranian students stormed the US embassy and took fifty-two Americans hostage (see: the Academy Award–winning movie *Argo*). As if a hostage crisis and an Iranian revolution weren't complicated enough, by 1980 the country also found itself at war with Iraq. The conflict was mostly geopolitical, with a long-standing border dispute between both nations. With the support of the United States (ahem), Iraq invaded Iran. At this point, the United States was politically motivated to back Iraq in the war. After Iran's revolution, the new regime was pushing hostile propaganda against the West. Iran was also gaining allies in the Middle East, and the US government worried the country would become the sole power in the region, thus wielding far too much influence. But guess what else happened in 1980?

I was born!

Yup, my life began during a hostage crisis, a revolution, and a war, which is why I didn't get to enter the world on my own time. My mom's labor had to be induced to avoid any risk of me being born during a bombing raid. Despite the tumult of the times, I was a happy, chubby baby who slept through the night and was loved by an extended family full of aunts, uncles, cousins, and grandmas. Most of my childhood photos include images of Samira and me, rolling around on intricate Persian rugs without a care in the world. We had no idea that our birthplace was in chaos and that mullahs were now running the country.

By 1982, with the hostage crisis finally over, but with no end in sight for the Iran-Iraq War or Khomeini's rule, my parents decided to peace out of the Middle East. They feared that Iran was never going to be the same again, and didn't want their children growing up without the freedoms they'd been afforded. There was only one problem: the borders were closed and no one was permitted to leave Iran. But my parents decided to take any means necessary to get us safely out of the country and to the United States. They chose the United States because they'd already lived there for a period of time, while my dad was in college. It also helped that my uncle had settled down in California and was willing to take us in. I suppose they had other options. They could have bided their time until the borders eventually reopened or gone through legal channels to get us green cards before we left Iran, but that would have likely taken years. With the country in upheaval, waiting would have meant putting their children's lives at risk—a gamble they weren't willing to take. Luckily, my dad had a friend with government ties who could secure us passports and special permission to leave the country, for a grand total of $15,000 (for my family, this was a small fortune). Only my mom (aged twenty-seven), my sister (aged five), and me (aged two) would apply to leave the country, since it was far more likely they'd grant us permission. If my dad were to have come along, the government would have assumed we were leaving our homeland for good. If he stayed behind in Iran, they figured my mom would return to her husband. The plan was that my baba would eventually find a way to follow us to America once it was safe for him to leave. In the back of their minds, I know they hoped the unrest in Iran would settle down, and we might be able to return to the country before our US visitor's visas expired.

Due to the perilous nature of our trip, we weren't allowed to inform family members we were leaving until the eve of our flight. I don't remember our departure, but I can only imagine what it was like for my grandmothers to hug and kiss their grandchildren farewell with no assurance that they'd ever see us again. My mom said good-bye to her husband of eight years and the love of her young life, neither of them wanting to acknowledge it could be months or years before they'd be reunited in America.

Looking back on the stories I've heard from that time, I often wonder how my maman survived it all. She left behind her home, her entire family, and her life partner in a war-torn country to give her children better opportunities. And even though she barely spoke English, she got us all to California (by way of Paris and Zurich, where we spent weeks trying to secure a US visitor's visa) in one piece. She's basically the Persian Wonder Woman. Once we arrived in the States, we squatted at my dayee* Mehrdad and aunt Geneva's house in Saratoga, California. My sister and I tried to find common ground with our half-American cousins, but that took a while to pan out. It didn't help that we'd infiltrated their space *and* that my sister's favorite pastime was sending me off to bite them. I guess the rumors are true. Undocumented immigrants are violent and dangerous.

The days without my dad were also seriously confusing for me as a two-year-old. My life was kind of like that children's book *Are You My Mother?*, where the lost baby bird tries to find its mom. I developed a habit of pointing to male mannequins in shopping malls and asking if they were my father. But three long months after we left Iran, my dad joined us in the Bay Area. The borders had reopened, and he left the country on a "business trip" to Italy. From there, he'd obtained a visitor's visa to the United States. But by the time my dad made it to America, I didn't recognize him. It would take weeks before I would agree to go near him. He says my sudden shyness was one of the most heartbreaking symptoms of being separated from us for so long. But at least we were back together, and our future in California was

---

Dayee means "uncle on your mom's side" in Farsi.

wide open. Once our visas expired, we applied for political asylum, but after two years without progress, we were told there was no record of our application. What followed was a series of messy, arduous, and complicated attempts at becoming US citizens. And a lifetime of figuring out how to fit in and be cool, without being a total traitor to my race.

God bless capitalism.

Lately, I've been so ready for Samira to go back to UC Davis. It's cool when she's away. I'll miss her, she'll come for a weekend, annoy me, then I'll miss her. I do love her so much, I adore her, I admire her, part of me wishes I was her without the bitchiness, without the stuck-up-ness, without the shallowness, and materialism. But who am I to judge?

—Diary entry: August 7, 1996

Chapter Two

* ★ *

Partners in Immigration Crime

I didn't grow up in a household where the word "hate" was banned from our vocabulary. My parents were far more offended by the word if it was uttered in English and not in our native Farsi, which they tried to encourage us to speak as much as possible. But regardless of the language it was articulated in, I'm not sure how anyone can survive life as a teen girl without dropping the occasional (or frequent) h-bomb. I felt things deeply, and I needed to express those feelings. For instance, I hated swimming during PE and considered it a basic human right to use my menstrual cycle as an excuse to stay out of the water. My PE teacher was a dude and missed the memo that tampons had been invented and that periods didn't last for three consecutive months. I also hated the fact that my parents permitted me to rollerblade only if I wore a helmet and kneepads. How was I supposed to look cute and athletic with such oppressive pieces of sporting equipment strapped to my body? But most of all, I *hated* my older sister, Samira. Sami was moody and bossy and didn't want to have anything to do with me. We fought over everything: who could control the TV remote, whose turn it was to use the phone, and who had dibs on marrying Leonardo DiCaprio. (Spoiler alert: neither of us grew up to be supermodels, so Leo was never an option.)

Our maman seemed mostly unfazed by the bitch-slapping, door slamming, and dramatic decreeing that we'd never speak to each other again. She encouraged us to love each other, but that was like asking Beyoncé and Becky with the Good Hair to hug it out.

"One day, you're going to be best friends. You'll see," she'd say with as much conviction as the Psychic Friends Network.

I worried these assertions could mean only one thing: my mom was secretly hitting the crack pipe. An affinity for street drugs was the only explanation for what were clearly the rantings of a strung-out lunatic.

"She will never be my best friend," I usually said in response. "I want her out of my life! FOREVER!"

No matter how regularly Samira and I brought each other to tears, my mom swore we'd grow up to realize we couldn't live without one another. But I wasn't buying the bill of goods Shohreh Saedi was selling. She didn't get it. She was the youngest of seven children and had three older sisters who adored her. I was confounded by their relationships. At one point, we even lived next door to one of my aunts and down the street from another . . . by choice. When you're a kid and live under the same roof as your siblings, you're forced to tolerate them. But why would anyone *choose* to live near their siblings if they don't have to? If that wasn't the definition of insanity, I didn't know what was.

But in typical wise-sage-mom fashion, she turned out to be right. The three-year age difference between Samira and me seemed insurmountable until my freshman year of high school. It was the fall of 1994 when we spent our days on the same campus for the first time since attending grade school together. The country was still reeling from Kurt Cobain's suicide and the infamous White Bronco chase. The only Kardashian we knew about was Rob Senior. Grunge music dominated the airwaves, with bands like Smashing Pumpkins, Pearl Jam, and Soundgarden performing mosh-pit-appropriate tracks. Flannels, goatees, and combat boots were in; bodysuits, Hypercolor, and perms were on their way out.

Samira was a senior at Lynbrook High School, and from the moment I enrolled as a ninth grader, her protective-older-sibling instincts kicked in and she took me under her wing. The junior high I'd opted to go to didn't feed into Lynbrook, but my parents insisted that I attend the same high school as my sister. Plus, Lynbrook (the alma mater of seven of my cousins) was one of the best public schools in the now-famous Silicon Valley, and even though my family couldn't afford to live in the district, we weren't going to let our less desirable zip code keep us down. Iranians are nothing if not resourceful. Since my dayee Mehrdad lived in the coveted and ritzy Saratoga neighborhood within Lynbrook's district, we used his address to finagle our way into the school. It was one of the many secrets that my sister and I kept from authorities. We weren't living in the country legally, and we weren't residents of the swanky Bay Area suburb our classmates lived in. If there was anything that terrified us as much as getting deported, it was that the principal's office would discover our address scam and send us down the road to the rough-and-tumble streets of Cupertino.

While our friends were in on our address fraud, my sister and I preferred not to advertise our undocumented immigrant status to them. I was too afraid of how girls who'd been born in America would judge me if I confessed that I wasn't supposed to be living in the country. There was one Canadian member of my clique, who always blathered on and on about how her parents had taken the appropriate legal channels to move to the United States. It wasn't fair that other people lived here illegally, she would say. I didn't bother pointing out that Canada wasn't in the throes of a war or revolution. Her family had the luxury of time on their side, because, well, their lives weren't in danger. I was also fairly certain if she learned about my illegal status, she would enlist her parents to call the proper authorities. I tried not to resent the fact that my friends were all allowed to live in the country. They may have had US passports, but at least I was the only one with the cool older sister.

To simply say Samira was "cool" would be the understatement of the century. My sister and her friends had reached legendary status at Lynbrook. They took #SquadGoals to epic heights. They were a group of eight girls, one prettier than the next. They had cool American names like Jocelyn and Rachel and Ann Marie. They were outgoing and confident, and transcended every high school clique. They had boyfriends who played guitar and sang in bands with names like Liquid Courage. I had a secret obsession with them that predated my days at Lynbrook. For years, I studied my sister's yearbooks and covertly read the messages her friends scribbled in the back pages. I knew who was dating whom. I knew everyone's high school crushes. I knew the names of hot senior guys I'd never met before. Seeing them in person was like being surrounded by my favorite celebrities. If Facebook and Instagram had existed back then, the rest of the school would have died of jealousy from the #NoFilter window into their social lives. I know I nearly did.

And though I'd studied them meticulously, I never quite understood my sister's goddess-like qualities until we walked the halls of Lynbrook together. She moved with a confidence that I had yet to master. She didn't need a green card to fit in. Everything about the way she carried herself said, "I belong." I wanted to bottle her poise and bathe in it daily. And when I walked alongside her, I ceased being known as Sara. High school seniors now solely referred to me as "Little Sami," and I wore the nickname like a badge of honor. I *was* Little Sami. To me, it was the highest of compliments.

I relished the mornings before school started. My sister

forbade me to have a first-period class, because she refused to drive me to campus at the crack of dawn, and I dutifully obliged. We lived in a two-story house, and my parents allowed us to take over the upstairs level. I realize now the proximity was just a clandestine plot to force us to like each other. Every morning, after getting ready for school, we hopped into Samira's beat-up gray 1988 Toyota Camry, which had been passed down to her from our parents. Live 105 regularly played on the radio as we made the fifteen-minute drive to school. With the windows down and Eddie Vedder singing "Sheets of empty canvas, untouched sheets of clay," we veered into the massive parking lot and snagged a spot in the front, where only the seniors were allowed to park. Even though I always got lost in the shuffle of tall, boisterous eighteen-year-olds, I loved moving through the quad with my sister. I wanted to stop time. I didn't want the school year to come to an end. I knew my life would turn to utter crap once the class of '95 graduated and I'd have to return to a state of complete anonymity.

But my freshman year of high school wasn't just a significant turning point in my relationship with Samira. It also marked a pivotal breakthrough in our immigration case. Back in 1984, when we learned that our applications for political asylum had mysteriously vanished, we decided to apply for what's called "adjustment of status," which is another (albeit slower) route to obtaining a green card. Since my dayee Mehrdad was an American citizen, he was able to sponsor our application for permanent residency. Through that appli-

26

cation, my sister and I each finally received an employment authorization card (also known as a "work permit"). The card allows noncitizens the opportunity to work in the United States, and it also enables them to acquire a Social Security number. In the pre–hostage crisis days, you could easily walk into the Social Security office, wait in line, fill out a form, and get a fancy blue card. But now we had to at least prove that we had a right to work in the country, and that was exactly what the employment authorization card stipulated. It had been only a year since I'd discovered we were undocumented, so I didn't quite grasp the gravity of the day our Social Security cards finally arrived in the mail. My diary entry from November 24, 1994, describes it as "the best day ever." A friend loaned me his Metallica CD, I flirted with my crush during an earthquake drill, I got an A on a science test, I didn't have to run much in PE, and:

> then, when I got home, I got my social security card in the mail . . . Days [of our Lives] was really good.

I gave the moment about as much weight as a strong episode of my favorite daytime drama. I had no idea the amount of legal fees and stress my parents endured in order for my sister and me to have government IDs. It had been twelve years since we moved to the States, and now the government finally knew I existed. This was both a relief and totally terrifying. If they knew I existed, then wouldn't it be easier for them to track me down and deport my ass? Surprisingly, the answer was no.

Unbeknownst to me, we were actually in a temporary "safe zone" from getting deported. Since our applications for green cards were "pending," the government wouldn't give us the boot, *unless* our application was denied.* So the stakes were still high. If at any point our application was rejected, we wouldn't be allowed to remain in the country. On the bright side, my sister and I were now legally allowed to work in the United States. Since immigrant children generally inherit their parents' insane work ethic, I was thrilled that I could finally make my own living.

My first legally paying gig was at a Baskin-Robbins within rollerblading distance of our house. I thought I'd hit pay dirt. I made $4.50 an hour to eat ice cream all day. I was in high school now, *and* I had my own job. I was an independent woman. My parents brought home the bacon, and I brought home two free scoops of Pralines 'N Cream every day. I finally felt like a grown-up. I was mature and worldly. I knew how to make a milk shake, and scooping ice cream gave me biceps to rival Michelle Obama's. The worst part of my day was being forced to wear a visor to work (the world's ugliest fashion accessory, second only to the fanny pack). But other than that, life was coming up roses.

And from where my sister was standing, I was no longer the bratty thorn in her side. I was now her contemporary. It

---

*The term "undocumented immigrant" includes anyone who is not a permanent resident of the country and does not have a visa to be here. Those with lawful permanent residency applications pending, and those who haven't filed any paperwork, are still considered "undocumented." It's important to remember that just because you file for a green card, there's no guarantee you will be granted one.

was obvious why I grew to love Samira once we went to high school together, but she also had reason to take a liking to me. Maybe it was the fact that on the mornings we entered campus together, I gawked at her like she was a movie star gracefully making her way down the red carpet. Or maybe it was the nights I kept her company when she received the devastating news that her friends had gone to a party without her. But mostly, it was my undying loyalty. Any of you younger siblings who are hoping to forge a better connection with your older brother or sister, here's all that's required of you: don't sell them out to Mom and Dad. There are exceptions to this rule, but I stuck by it pretty hard.

As a child, I relished reporting my sister's screwups to my parents. Like the time she called 911 just for kicks—with no thought to the fact that we were a household of undocumented immigrants—and the police showed up at our front door. We said we dialed the number by accident, and the police let us off the hook with a warning. When I wasn't telling on Samira, I would regularly resort to blackmail, extortion, or torture. I suppose if SAVAK still existed in Iran, they could have hired me to be their first ten-year-old agent. I remember one particular weekend morning when my dad forced me to walk to the grocery store to buy my sister ginger ale, since she had a stomach virus. A virus? Ha. I could smell her hangover from a mile away. I cursed her under my breath as I carried the heavy liters of soda home, and even though she couldn't keep any food down, I ate a stinky omelet in her presence. I'd seen the trick on a rerun of *Roseanne* when Darlene tormented a hungover Becky.

But once we went to the same school, I learned a very important lesson: Samira was far more valuable to me than my parents. They didn't have the power to improve my social status. So my loyalties lay with my sister. I had to let her know that I could be trusted. I would do anything to demonstrate my allegiance. I kept every illicit activity to myself. I didn't tell my parents when she'd cut school to go to the beach, or that she once missed an entire Aerosmith concert because she passed out from drinking before the band took the stage.

But a year or so later, when Samira was in college, I reluctantly agreed to keep her most severe act of rebellion to myself. When she revealed to me she was taking a secret trip to Mexico with her friends, I didn't say, "But you *know* that we don't have green cards, and we're not allowed to leave the country. If you get stopped at the border, they could detain you. Worst-case scenario: They might send you to Iran, and then no one will be around to loan me cool outfits and drive me around town. Or you might have to live in Mexico forever, and you took French in high school." Instead, I said something like: "That's so awesome. Bring me back a souvenir. ¡*Hasta luego!*"

I knew better than to give her a lecture. Besides, her friends had assured her that they checked driver's licenses only when you crossed into Mexico. How could girls with perfect hair and a closetful of stylish flannels from Hot Topic be wrong about anything? Clearly, they knew how Border Patrol operated. They were the original girl squad. There was no way they'd let one of their own get deported.

But during the few days my parents thought my sister was safely within our country's borders in San Diego, I was terrified for her. How would I be able to look my parents in the eye if something happened? It was like being stuck between a rock and Ryan Gosling's chiseled abs. If I took the responsible route and told my parents the truth, my sister would never speak to me again, and I'd never get to party with her in college. There was too much on the line. I had way too much to lose. If I had to live out the rest of my years sending letters to a Mexican prison, I could handle it. My parents would never have to know that I aided and abetted her bad behavior. After all, wasn't that a younger sibling's primary reason for living? I was the Solange to her Beyoncé. The Serena to her Venus. The Pippa to her Kate. I was *not* the Fredo to her Michael Corleone. Not just because Fredo was older, but because he betrayed Michael. And Michael had him killed.

My sister did make it back across the border, and my parents were none the wiser. And I'd finally proven myself to be a trusted servant. But if the secret Mexico trip was the defining test of my loyalty, I really earned my stripes when my sister and her best friend turned me into a legitimate stalker. I'll call my sister's friend Claudia* to protect her identity. Claudia had a longtime crush on a guy named Connor, pining

---

*All names have been changed, with the exception of those of close family members.

for him through most of high school and at the start of college. After a series of flirtatious phone calls, it seemed like Claudia and Connor's time had finally arrived. They'd both returned home for Thanksgiving with the understanding that their love would be consummated. Or that they would make out and hold hands. But Connor was suddenly acting weird. He wouldn't return Claudia's calls and wouldn't commit to any of the plans they'd made leading up to the visit. It didn't matter that it was almost midnight when my sister and Claudia filled me in on the Connor Affair. There was only one solution: we had to drive by his house on the other side of town and see what the guy was hiding.

Keep in mind that this is before the Internet was in every household (seriously) and we didn't have the luxury of cyberstalking. If you wanted to invade someone's privacy, you couldn't do it easily from the safety of your computer. You had to have enormous balls to track someone's every move, and I was about to grow a pair. Samira, of course, was the mastermind of the entire operation. The plan was as follows: We would drive by Connor's house, and if anything seemed fishy, we would park down the block. I would get out of the car, make the long walk to his house, knock on his door, and recite everything my sister had directed me to say.

"You have to pretend to be really upset," Samira added as we turned down his street. When we slowly inched past his house, Claudia noticed an unidentified white Jetta in the driveway (a car that could be driven only by a female), and that was our cue. We had no choice. We had to carry out the plan. They parked down the street and wished me luck, and I quietly slipped out of the car.

Be brave, I told myself as I made the agonizingly long walk in the pitch-black to his driveway. I could do this. I was a badass. I was Little Sami. If I could lie to the American government, then I could con my way through a conversation with some shady college kid. There was only one problem: Connor wasn't just some college kid. After years of studying my sister's yearbooks, I knew him from afar. I knew he was a ravishing ginger with perfect dimples and an irresistible smile. Even though he'd graduated from Lynbrook before I enrolled, he was the kind of guy who was still talked about in the hallways.

Once I arrived at the front door, I took a deep breath and knocked. The door swung open, and Connor stood in the entryway . . . with his bare chest on display. He smiled at me. I tried to resist his charms and not smile back. For a brief moment, I imagined telling him this was a setup and I'd been forced by my mentally unstable sister and her clingy friend to harass him. He'd invite me in for a hot cocoa, praise me for my honesty, and then we'd fall in love and run away together. Claudia would eventually understand. But I didn't do that.

"Hi," I said shyly. "Um, I live down the street, and my dog got loose, and I can't find him. I was wondering if maybe you heard anything?"

Connor gave me a sympathetic shrug, and said he hadn't. He asked what kind of dog I owned, and the first breed that came to mind was a Chihuahua. I could tell I'd given a convincing performance by the way he assured me that he'd keep his eyes peeled for my scared, lost, fake dog. Just as I turned to leave, I heard a girl's voice from inside ask him who was at the door. I did not give in to my sudden urge to kick him in the nuts, call him a jerk, and berate him for lying to sweet Claudia with the perfect tan and ridiculously long legs. Instead, I made my way down his front steps. The walk back to the car was even more excruciating than the walk to Connor's door. Nowhere in the little-sister job requirements did it say that I had to break the heart of one of the VIP members of the girl squad. I slid into the back seat and announced, "He didn't have his shirt on and I heard a girl's voice inside the house."

I was only fifteen, but even I knew what this meant. They were totally boning. Claudia didn't cry when I confirmed her worst fear, but I could tell from the shaky tone of her voice that she was wounded. My sister consoled her all the way home, and we agreed that Connor was a pasty dick. We also agreed that I was the coolest little sister for going through with the plan in the first place.

But despite their praise, I was never as brave as Samira. I'm still not. I didn't like to break the rules. I would have never gone to Mexico when I was undocumented. I wasn't as good at speaking my mind as she was, or as quick on my feet in a crisis. Samira Saedi was tough. She gave zero fucks before that was a meme. If it had been my sister at Connor's door, she'd have pushed herself into his house and told the girl who was sitting inside that he was a two-timer. She was my hero, and that night, a tiny bit of her power and glory rubbed off on me. I hated that in a couple of days she'd be going back to college and I'd be getting ready for school Monday morning without her.

My mom *had* seen into the future and she was right. We were best friends. It felt as though we couldn't live without each other, and that was why a few months prior, I'd sobbed during her high school graduation, flung myself onto the stage, grabbed hold of her legs, and screamed "NEVER LEAVE ME" while she accepted her diploma. Okay, that's maybe a slight exaggeration. But without her, I knew I would no longer be Little Sami. I would no longer confidently stride through the senior parking lot. Instead, I'd be dropped off

Sisterly love.

in the bus circle by my dad with the rest of the nerds. Even worse, I knew it was the end of an era. With my sister away at college, our family of five would never live under the same roof together again. The other upstairs bedroom would be empty. I didn't care if I would have the bathroom to myself, because it would mean losing my better half.

For most of my childhood, my sister brought me to hysterics from fights and days of the silent treatment. Back when we shared a room, she was the one who'd divide up the floor with masking tape, building an invisible wall between us. But the day we dropped her off at UC Davis, she once again threw me into an emotional tailspin. I didn't want to go from being the middle child to the oldest kid in the house. I kept it together throughout the whole day. My smile didn't waver when we met her college roommate and helped set up her dorm room. I managed to stay upbeat when we explored the town and ate lunch together as a family. But the moment we dropped her off for good, I turned into a complete puddle. And she cried, too. Because that's what happens when you feel that connected to someone. They laugh and you laugh. You cry and they cry. More than twenty years later, my sister still has the same effect on me. She lives in Northern California with her family, and I live in Los Angeles with mine . . . but if it were up to me, we'd take a page from my mom and aunt's book and live next door to each other.

FREQUENTLY ASKED QUESTION #1
What's the difference between being Persian and being Iranian?

Essentially, there isn't much separating the two. I'll be using them interchangeably, because when you're writing a book it's nice to use different words to say the same thing. Technically speaking, Persian is an ethnicity, while Iranian is a nationality. So you may be from Iran, but you could be Kurdish instead of Persian.

But the country was also formally called Persia until the government changed the name to Iran in 1935. By 1959, scholars convinced the government that Persia and Iran should both be part of the vernacular.

When people inquire about my ethnicity, I prefer to say that I'm Iranian. It always feels like "Persian" is the more pretentious response, and a term to use when you don't want people to associate you with a country that's been referred to as part of the axis of evil. But to anyone who still refers to Iran in those terms, I respectfully say: stop being a horrible xenophobe.

It's like every time I walk by him, I have a tinge of hope that this could be it. He might talk to me or bump into me or whatever, but when nothing ever happens when he walks by, he takes a little piece of my heart with him.

—Diary entry: December 3, 1994

Chapter Three

◆ ★ ◆

Sporting the Frida Kahlo

The comment left me adrift in a river of teen angst. Words escaped me. For once, I didn't have a cutting response at the ready. My face was on fire. My eyes filled with hot tears. I wanted to crawl under my wobbly desk in ninth-grade English and stay hidden there forever. It wasn't the worst plan. Our high school was equipped with showers and a well-stocked cafeteria. I could remain tucked away on the floor of Mrs. Carter's classroom until the final bell rang, and when everyone left to go home, I could emerge from hiding to eat the leftover scraps in the commissary kitchen and shower in the girls' locker room. I'd let the warm water run over me as I cradled myself in the fetal position. I'd sleep on the cot in the nurse's office, and when morning rolled around, I'd find safe harbor beneath another desk so that I would never have to make eye contact with anyone again. I would miss my parents, but then again, they were the ones to blame for my predicament.

"You did this to me!" I would scream if they tried to take me home. "You're the reason I have to live the rest of my days like Quasimodo's busted little sister."

Unless you make your living as a supermodel, you know what it's like to have at least one physical imperfection that makes you feel irreversibly ugly. That one feature you'd change in a heartbeat if you could. For me, it's always been my dominant nose. Why couldn't I have been the first Iranian in the history of the world born with a button nose? Why did my face have to confirm the most widespread stereotype about our people? But it wasn't my unfortunate nasal structure that nearly turned me into a hermit the day I decided to build a home under my desk. It was a tiny patch of unwanted hair that had never even made it onto my "Ten Things I Hate About Myself" list, until Gideon Wright pointed it out.

Gideon was my very first high school crush. The pages of my freshman-year diary are littered with his name. My love for him vacillated from one entry to another. Some days, I wanted to be with him forever. Other days, I knew my feelings would never be reciprocated and that it was my civic feminist duty to get over him. I didn't know any of the other boys in our freshman class, and Gideon was the only guy I'd come across who not only was cute and charming but also appreciated my dry humor. I fell for him by default. We sat next to each other in English, and even though he was way out of my league, a part of me clung to the hope that my dazzling personality and biting sense of humor would wear him down. The beginning of our relationship would play out like the end of every good teen movie where the popular guy falls for the nerdy girl. I imagined that Gideon would proudly hold my hand through the halls of our high school and announce to his football player buddies that he was into me and that he wasn't going to hide it anymore. Those were the kinds of fantasies that monopolized my thoughts at night . . . and during the day . . . and in the morning . . . and at dusk.

Here's what I never imagined Gideon doing in those fantasies: snickering at me in class and declaring, "You only have ONE eyebrow."

It took me a moment to fully comprehend what he was saying. I had two eyebrows, just like everyone else. And then I realized he was referring to the thin strands of hair that existed between them. I'd been cursed with a unibrow. How had I never realized it before? I never thought it was that noticeable. My whole life, my mom and aunts had praised me for how American I looked. It was a virtue to have paler skin than most Iranians, not to mention hair that was several shades lighter than my family members'. The dense hair on my arms was almost blond, and my eyebrow hairs weren't nearly as thick as the ones my sister had been born with. If she was blessed with flawless skin and a great rack, then I was blessed with unwanted hair that was less visible in the sun. My unibrow being made fun of wasn't part of the love story I'd envisioned for Gideon and me. I'd expect that from the shallow, pompous best-friend character who would try to get between us, but not from the guy I was supposed to end up with before the credits rolled.

I went home that day and examined my eyebrows in the mirror. Good God, they were awful. I took another look at my school portrait and discovered that I looked like I had a hungry, fuzzy caterpillar sprawled across my face. That's when I had an epiphany: when my mom and aunts praised me for being hairless . . . they meant by *Persian* woman standards. I was still hairy by everyone else's standards. Why didn't any of my "no hair, don't care" Asian friends or my fair-skinned, blond American friends take me aside and say, "Sara, if you want to have sex with anyone ever, then you might want to consider purchasing tweezers and separating your Siamese eyebrows from each other"?

But even if they had, it wouldn't have made a difference. Believe it or not, plucking your eyebrows is considered a rite of passage for Iranian girls. According to my mom, we couldn't mess with our brows until we turned fifteen. We were, however, allowed to shave our legs and bleach our mustaches. (I mean, the woman wasn't a monster.)

Freshman-year school portrait.

44

But that meant I still had one very long and torturous year before I stopped being Fuzzy Caterpillar Forehead Girl. There was no way Gideon would publicly call me his girlfriend if I didn't pluck the ten to fifteen hairs that were ruining my life. Danny Zuko didn't want to be seen with Sandy because she wore cardigans. *Grease* would have had a very different ending if she'd shown up at that carnival in spandex, a head of curls, and a bushy unibrow.

I didn't understand why my mom insisted on making me suffer. Didn't she know that all the other girls in my freshman class were sporting the coveted and trendy two-eyebrow look?

"Trust me," my maman would say, "once you start plucking your eyebrows, you'll never be able to stop."

But even if my mom backed off and let me pluck the unwanted hairs, I knew I couldn't show up to school the very next day with stand-alone eyebrows. Gideon would know that he'd been the reason for the cosmetic change. I may have been in love with him, and I may have thought he was way too good for me, but I still had enough pride and dignity to know that I couldn't show him that he had that much power over me. I had to play it cool and keep my unibrow proudly on display. It was okay to cry in the privacy of my own bedroom, but I would never let him see me crumble. Life would have to go on relatively unchanged. I would forge ahead. I would continue to manage my upper-lip hair, and do my best not to constantly run my finger over the tiny patch of hair that was destroying my will to live.

Despite my plan, I still couldn't understand why Iranian societal norms dictated an age-appropriate time to shape one's eyebrows. I'd already accepted that Persians cared the most about (1) family and (2) how extended family members perceived them. The latter splintered into a whole slew of issues. Appearances were everything in our culture. How much money we appeared to have, how we dressed, how much we weighed, what we looked like—the list goes on. In a family of immigrants where the Saedis were essentially the only ones who hadn't been granted permanent residency, we were already at a disadvantage. There were only a few things that could help us save face, and that included keeping a nice house and looking our best. I had optimum success with the former. My bedroom was decked out in white wicker furniture and a trendy daybed. My decorating aesthetic included a poster of the earth with the tagline "Save the Humans." Another wall included the iconic photo of a gingerbread man with the description "The Perfect Man (He's Quiet, He's Sweet, and If He Gives You Any Grief, You Can Bite His Head Off)." My bedroom perfectly encapsulated my personality. It said: Here's a girl who cares about the environment but also has an irreverent sense of humor. Who wouldn't want to hang out with her?

But my physical appearance was a different story. I had always been short for my age. Nicknames like "Shrimp" and "Small Fry" haunted me through grade school. In high school, my petite frame and height didn't seem to matter quite as much. I still envied my statuesque friends (my closest girlfriends were five ten; I was barely five feet), but I'd come to accept my vertical limitations. My wardrobe left something to be desired at the start of ninth grade. My go-to outfit was a white polo shirt, khaki corduroy pants, a denim jacket, and a pair of navy-blue Converse. I dressed like a pre-pubescent boy. Plus, I still had a mouthful of braces, a nose my face would never grow into, and ears that stuck out if I didn't cover them up with my frizzy brown hair. I definitely fit the description of the ugly duckling in makeover movies, except that those girls were actually gorgeous actresses disguised by poorly framed glasses.

I wasn't always the awkward and dorky girl. I am not too modest to admit that in sixth grade, I had serious game. Boys liked me. Boys fought over me. I was like the Gigi Hadid of De Vargas Elementary. This was before I hit puberty. Actually, it was before anyone in my school hit puberty. Except for a few early developers, no one had boobs. Not only was I undeniably adorable, I was also the student body president of our elementary school. Yeah, I was an *undocumented immigrant* who'd been elected to public office. How do you like me now, ICE?* In three adjectives, I was pretty and smart and popular. In fact, I've never had as much confidence as I did when I was eleven. Everything was going my way. My crush actually liked me back, and when I asked him to "go" with me, he said yes. That's right. I was so self-assured that

*ICE stands for Immigration and Customs Enforcement. The agency, created in the wake of the events of September 11, 2001, is in charge of implementing our country's immigration laws. In other words, they're the people who will deport you.

I wasn't biding my time, waiting for boys to ask me out. I was taking the bull by the horns. At this point, I was also ignorant of our illegal immigration status and the sad fact that the government could kick my family and me out of the country, effectively ending any relationship I started. Life was simple and uncomplicated.

But it all changed when I graduated from sixth grade and enrolled in a junior high that accommodated several different elementary schools. Puberty hit fast and hard, and I went from a solid ten to a solid six. I couldn't compete with girls from other grade schools who had perfectly styled perms and brand-new boobs. I couldn't pull off baggy pants and tight bodysuits. No one seemed to think my plaid blazer and matching headband were cool (I was the Blair Waldorf of my generation). My stock plummeted, and by high school, it plateaued. Oh, and my hot sixth-grade boyfriend left me for a girl who could effortlessly pull off an oversize Dallas Cowboys parka.

Some days, it felt like I was letting my mom down. She was, and still is, a total knockout. Mama Saedi's delicate features, stylish short hair, youthful skin, and radiant smile were regularly commented upon. My mom fit in the MILF category. My friends and *their* moms were always pointing out the fact that I had a pretty mom, but they never followed up the comment by saying I resembled her. And still, I was proud of my mom's good looks. Even though none of her genes had apparently been passed down to me, I felt like it gave me a certain cachet among my girlfriends to have the gorgeous mom. I didn't even find it disturbing when guys my age would openly say they thought my mom was hot. You'd think an ultra-attractive mother like mine would understand why my appearance was hampered by my Frida Kahlo eyebrows, coupled with my inability to paint stunning self-portraits of said eyebrows.

But my mom didn't understand. You want to know why?

Because she was afraid of what our relatives would think if word got out that Shohreh let her daughter pluck her brows before she'd turned fifteen. Would the older generation of great-aunts and great-uncles think she was a bad mom? Would they infer that her kids were sluts and harlots? Would her sisters scoff at her for abandoning her Iranian ideals and allowing hair-free Americans to weaken her resolve? Probably. My parents will be the first to admit that a favorite Iranian pastime is to sit in judgment of others. We go to family parties not to bask in each other's presence but to whisper among ourselves about tacky dresses, botched plastic surgery, and disastrous haircuts and highlights. (Iranian women who dyed their hair blond were just setting themselves up for a lifetime of ridicule.) If anyone could replace the late Joan Rivers on the red carpet, it'd be a Persian woman. Those bitches are brutal.

So you can understand my mom's conundrum. If she allowed her daughter to flirt with hair removal, then family members would whisper about it. If she made her daughter stick to the natural, overgrown eyebrow look, then family members would whisper about it. Either way, my poor maman was in a lose-lose situation. I'd be remiss not to add that she was also the type of mom who thought I looked beautiful no matter what, and regularly told me so. But I didn't care if the powerful and wise lioness who had given me life thought I was pretty. I wanted the fourteen-year-old boy who was completely blind to my inner beauty to give me validation. Luckily, after enough time passed from the Unibrow Burn of 1994, and after Samira appealed to our mom on my behalf, she finally gave in. I was awarded tweezers and a small boost to my fragile self-esteem.

Sayonara, suckers, I thought as I pulled out every last hair that bridged my eyebrows to each other. The pain stung and my skin turned red, but it was completely worth it. My mom had tried to warn me that once I started plucking, there would be no going back. I had crossed over to the dark side of hair removal. I had entered the endless abyss of threading and waxing and lasers—otherwise known as a lifetime of physical and psychological torture. But I welcomed the agony.

Gideon never came around. My unibrow was plucked on the daily, but it didn't change anything between us. He was still just that guy I occasionally flirted with in English class. Maybe it never occurred to him to think anything more of me. Or maybe he was secretly charmed by my relentless sass but didn't have the guts to pursue me if the popular crowd didn't approve.

"If a boy teases you, it means he likes you." Everyone always makes this assumption, but in my case it didn't pan out. The only outcome from the teasing was my seriously damaged sense of self, and if I'm going to be truthful, not even tweezers helped repair it. In the back of my mind, I lived in fear that being Middle Eastern was considered a turnoff to boys my age. No one at my high school knew much about Iran and mostly associated my culture with terrorism and magic carpets. I wasn't one of the desirable exotic races (Asians did very well at my high school—they also made up 60 percent of the student body), and I wasn't the all-American cheerleader type, either. Even my prettier older sister never seemed to have boyfriends, when all the other white girls in her clique did. I couldn't help but wonder if my race automatically put me at a disadvantage. It didn't matter how often my mom told me I was beautiful, because I knew the truth: I had peaked in sixth grade.

February 8, 1995

I feel so ugly. There must be something really wrong with me. All the guys like all the made-up, permed hair, easy, trendy girls. And I really refuse to change my whole personality to be liked by guys. I know I'm not disgusting. I guess I'm pretty average. I just feel so inexperienced, and I'm sure it shows. Sometimes I just wish I could get in people's heads and see what they think about me. I've never felt like such a loser before.

Today, I wish I could travel back to 1995 and slap some sense into the old me. I would grab me by the shoulders and explain that it was great that I felt different, and that I was far better than average. I would tell me that low self-esteem would be my biggest obstacle in life, and that I had to dig deep and do better than phrases of encouragement like "I know I'm not disgusting." Mostly, I would tell me that Gideon Wright wouldn't amount to much in the future anyway. I can't even find the guy on Facebook, so clearly he has nothing great going on that he wants to brag about to hundreds of acquaintances. And finally, I would end with one parting thought: just because a girl has a perm, it does not mean that she's easy. It just means that she's going to have a lifetime of very damaged hair.

My parents want to read one of my journals so bad. They keep asking me to let them read one. They don't understand that these are so personal. I don't even write huge stuff in here, just everyday crap, but it's basically everything I'm thinking in my head. Most of the stuff looks lame and corny when I look back on it, but they're only for me, no one else. . . . I could see them reading one anyway.

—Diary entry: June 17, 1996

Chapter Four

—— ◆ ★ ◆ ——

The Myth of the Iranian Parent

If my parents were a pie chart, they would look a little something like this one.

And yet one might assume strict, conservative, diabolical monsters with foreign accents raised me. Only the foreign-

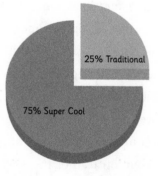

25% Traditional

75% Super Cool

accent part of that statement is true. My mom and dad defied (most of) the stereotypes regularly associated with Persian parents. This chapter would probably have a whole lot more conflict if Ali and Shohreh Saedi were more like Andre Agassi's militant Tehran-raised dad (and I might be a tennis champion today), but I was raised by open-minded liberals whose philosophies on parenting boiled down to these three words:

"We trust you."

But for anyone who's more familiar with the strict-foreign-parent archetype in popular culture, let's break down the stereotypes associated with Persian moms and dads.

— Stereotype 1 —
Persian parents allow their kids to choose from only four occupations: doctor, lawyer, dentist, and engineer.

Ethnic background aside, most parents would be immensely proud if their children pursued any of the above occupations. They're stable, lucrative, and highly respectable professions. But my parents didn't have hard-and-fast rules about our career aspirations. One of the many downsides of emigrating from one country to another is that you're not always left with the option to follow your dreams. My dad had a degree in mechanical engineering from Louisiana State University, but since he was undocumented, it was impossible for him to get hired for jobs that fit his qualifications. My mom's biggest regret in life was that she never went to college. Even in the pre-revolution Iran of the 1970s, higher education wasn't exactly a priority for women. She married young, threw herself into motherhood, and had to adjust to a new culture and language when she moved to America. Enrolling in college was a luxury she couldn't afford. In the early days of living here, she went from working at a local Sizzler to becoming a nanny. Eventually, she joined my dad to help manage their small business.

Peninsula Luggage was a sales and repair shop in San Mateo,

a town about thirty miles north of where we lived. It was owned and operated by my uncles, but when they moved on to start a home-appraisal business, my dad bought them out.

My parents ran the shop together. It wasn't what they imagined doing with their lives, but they needed an income to pay the rent and to save enough money to buy a house one day. Even though I helped them out some weekends (for a measly three dollars an hour—under the table, because I was an undocumented immigrant), they never expected their kids to follow in their footsteps. Growing up in the United States meant we, unlike our parents, had the privilege of exploring what, if anything, we were passionate about.

My parents, the proud small-business owners.

"This is America," they'd say. "You can do anything you set your mind to."

I'm not positive that the word "anything" included an acting career, but by high school, I was convinced that being in movies was my destiny. You know how some celebrities wax poetic in interviews about how they just knew they'd be famous? Well, that's how I felt, too. My parents didn't seem to blink an eye when I informed them of my future plans, though it's entirely possible they had to excuse themselves from the room so they could giggle hysterically at me in private.

"She thinks she can be *an actress*? Muahahahahaha."

They knew I had an unhealthy obsession with movies and television shows, and they were partially to blame. They seemed to have little concept of what was inappropriate to show to an eight-year-old. In second grade, my mom took me to the theater to see R-rated films like *Rain Man* and *Cocktail*. I was probably the only child in America who was horrified when Dustin Hoffman forgot to thank Tom Cruise in his Oscar acceptance speech for best actor back in 1989.

I'm also relatively certain other teenagers in my neighborhood did not wake up at 5:00 in the morning, along with publicists and studio heads, just so they could watch the Oscar nominations announced live. When a school camping trip to Yosemite conflicted with the Academy Awards, I briefly considered starting a petition to have the trip postponed, but my mom promised me she'd tape the broadcast. Yes, before the DVR was invented, we actually had to insert a VHS tape into a VCR in order to record anything we wouldn't be home to watch.

Times were really tough (especially since no one actually understood how to program their VCRs). From then on, I was allowed to skip school on the day of the Oscars (which was a Monday back then), because I considered it a national holiday.

Truth be told, I don't know if I was as fascinated with acting as much as I was with the cult of celebrity. More specifically, the world of Winona Ryder. During my teen years, she was my number one girl crush. You may know her as the mom from *Stranger Things,* but in the nineties, Winona was the "it" girl. She was as iconic as Jennifer Lawrence is today. She dated guys like Johnny Depp and Matt Damon. She was a modern-day Audrey Hepburn, with the delicate features necessary to pull off a pixie cut. I once spotted her at a U2 concert in Oakland and literally screamed at the top of my lungs: "Winona, I love you. Winona, I want to be you." She scurried away as quickly as possible.

I was convinced that one day, little old Persian me would get famous and I would get to play her younger, less attractive, somewhat ethnically ambiguous sister in movies. If you're too young to comprehend the power of Winona, then I suggest you stream the following movies immediately after finishing this book:

1. *Heathers*
2. *Welcome Home, Roxy Carmichael*
3. *Edward Scissorhands*
4. *Mermaids*
5. *Reality Bites*

The best part about Winona was that she lived in San Francisco and grew up in the Bay Area just like me. We were homies. When I read an interview with her in *Vogue* that mentioned she got her start at the A.C.T. Young Conservatory in San Francisco, I decided that I was destined to follow in her footsteps.

And my parents were like: "Cool, we'll pay for that even though we totally can't afford it. Follow your pipe dream, honey! Yay, America!"

For most of my childhood, I thought all dads worked six days a week, but I began to notice that most of my friends' fathers took Saturdays and Sundays off. When I asked to take acting classes in San Francisco, my dad didn't point out the fact that he already commuted forty minutes to work each day, and that this would mean driving me an hour into the city on his only day off. He seemed excited to spend the quality father-daughter time together in the car, and waited around in the city until I got out of class. I decided to make a note of that sacrifice so that I could reference it in my future poignant Oscar acceptance speech. But before we could shell out the four hundred dollars for classes at A.C.T. Young Conservatory, I had to go through an intense interview process (with one guy who probably let anyone into the program who wasn't a complete psychopath and could afford to pay the tuition fee). I wasn't nervous for my interview. Even though I moved through high school like a puppy lost in a coyote den, I had less fear of adults. I liked to think I had an old soul.

So it was no surprise to me that I hit it off with the head of the program. I tried to act normal as he told me stories about Winona. He described her as "luminous" and said that he could tell she was a star from the moment they met. I imagined that in a few years, he'd be sharing the same stories about me. When I left the building and waited on a bustling street corner in Union Square for my dad to pick me up, I felt like I had found my true calling. Being in San Francisco made me feel like I could conquer the world. No one at my high school knew it, but I wasn't meant to live in the suburbs. I belonged in a city with a constant stream of traffic noise, busy pedestrians, and musicians busking on the sidewalk. *This*, I thought to myself. *This* is why the revolution in Iran happened. So I could move to America and become the most famous Persian actress alive. The night after my interview, we ordered Chinese food and my fortune read as follows:

"The star of riches is shining upon you."

I carefully taped it into my journal for added inspiration. One day, I would look at it and think, Daaaamn, fortune cookie! You were spot-on!

But here's what my parents actually helped me discover by driving me to theater school every week: I totally sucked at acting. How did celebrities make it seem so easy? There were kids in my class who'd been taking courses at A.C.T. since they were toddlers. They could do Swahili accents and had mastered the Claire Danes chin tremble on cue. They thought improv games were *fun,* and dropped lines from Tennessee Williams plays in casual conversation. I was just there to get famous and win an Oscar someday. The most riveting performance I gave during the twelve-week session was portraying a stoner at a party. I suddenly began dreading the drive into the city. So when the course ended, I didn't sign up for more classes. I'd walked away learning a very important lesson: it's no fun to do things you're crappy at.

If my parents hadn't gone out of their way to let me take acting classes, then it would have taken me much longer to learn I was more comfortable (and hopefully more competent) as a writer. My mom and dad failed to point out that writing wasn't exactly the most stable career, either. Some might say they were supportive to a fault. To prove it, here's a cringe-worthy (and terribly written) diary excerpt:

March 7, 1997
The other night, my dad told me to write something in my journal. He told me to write: "Tonight at 9:28 p.m. on March 5, my dad told me I would be successful." Who knows.

— Stereotype 2 —
Iranian parents are REALLY strict.

Like most immigrant parents, my mom and dad made it abundantly clear they had high expectations of their offspring. A common refrain in our household was "We didn't move all the way to this country so you could _____." Fill in the blank with any number of deeds: *get C's on your report card, talk back to us,* or *leave the house dressed like a cheap hooker.* We had a curfew set for 11:30 p.m. and were always told to call whenever we arrived at our intended destination. But we were also permitted to leave the house and go to parties and sleepovers. It might not be the most popular parenting style, but they really believed if they trusted our judgment, then we wouldn't have the urge to rebel. My sister was the resident troublemaker in the house, but even she was tame compared to most teenagers. She drank and smoked pot occasionally, but she was also an A student and widely known as the most responsible girl in the squad. The one who was most likely to help her friends after they'd passed out from a night of drinking (okay, except at that Aerosmith concert), and the person who usually volunteered to be designated driver.

Most of my American friends had way stricter rules in their households. For instance, my best friend, Izzy, wasn't allowed to spend the night at my place, because her mom felt there wasn't enough adult supervision in the Saedi home. That wasn't entirely untrue. My parents were social creatures, and they figured if I had a friend spending the night and keeping me busy, it gave them the perfect opportunity to go to a nice dinner at the Olive Garden or bust a move at a family party. After all, they trusted me.

But really, my parents abandoned everything they knew and loved because they didn't want their daughters to grow up with a strict religious code. Why inflict the same rules on us in America? They wanted us to cruise through the quaint streets of downtown Los Gatos with friends. They wanted us to go to dances and parties that included members of the opposite sex. They were okay if we drank, as long as we drank responsibly and never drove. Most of all, they wanted us to take advantage of every opportunity afforded to us by living in the United States.

In my not-so-humble opinion, I believe that immigrants are the true American patriots. We never take living in this country for granted. We still had family in Iran, and we knew how complicated and difficult their lives were under the new regime. Back then, we heard stories of teenagers who were beaten by the police for attending a coed party. My own cousin was arrested and whipped by police for getting caught socializing with the opposite sex. They detained him until my aunt and uncle bribed the police for his release. And that's precisely why my baba and maman tried to give us the space to live our lives. Why bring their kids to America, and not let them enjoy the freedoms they wouldn't have been permitted in Iran?

— Stereotype 3 —
Iranian parents are conservative zealots.

Yes and no. My parents were terrified by the thought of their daughters dating, making out with boys, or—God forbid—being sexually active. These were rights they didn't think I needed from the tender age of fourteen to twenty-five. But even when it came to talks of dating or future spouses, my sister and I were never pressured to marry someone Iranian.

My parents knew the dating pool was already small enough and that the only way we'd connect with an Iranian guy was if he'd been raised in America like us. They loved the idea of a guy entering our family who could speak Farsi, but they even warned us against future Iranian in-laws.

"They're too involved with their kids," my maman would say. "They'll just try to stick their noses in your business. You're better off marrying someone American." This was a huge relief, since I had officially moved on from Leonardo DiCaprio and had plans to spend the rest of my life with Ethan Hawke.

My parents also considered themselves atheists and raised us as such. They were both brought up Muslim but came to America as infidels. In their opinion, religious rule had damaged the country they once loved. Even though they would say things like *Khoda nakoneh* (God forbid) and *Inshallah* (God willing) and *Cheghad Khoda Rahm Kard* (God was really watching out for us), they didn't necessarily believe in God or Allah. And they also didn't understand why we had so many friends who tried to convert us into becoming Christians.

When my brother was five, he returned from a church barbecue he'd attended with a friend and announced "Jesus is in my bones." My dad was like: "Um, no. Jesus is not in your bones. Marrow is in your bones, and calcium and collagen." I knew my parents respected other people's beliefs, but they also considered religion a way to comfort oneself from the inevitable: the eternal abyss of nothingness, obviously. Which is why I had a habit of debating my most religious friends in high school. I couldn't believe they thought I was going to go to hell unless I accepted Jesus Christ as my Lord and Savior.

"But I'm a really good person," I would remind them.

"All we can do is just pray for you," they'd respond.

"Fine, while you're at it—pray that my boobs come in, and that a halfway decent-looking boy with a good heart and kind hands will want to touch them," I was tempted to respond.

But they did more than pray for me. They actually tried to convert me. It almost worked, thanks to the undeniably holy powers of a hot guy with a skateboard. Our near romance started when one of my best friends, Rebecca, invited me to go to a weekend sleepaway camp with her youth group. She promised it wouldn't be overly religious, so I agreed to check it out. She lied (which I'm pretty sure was against her religion). It turned out I had signed up for a weekend of prayer and singing hymns about Jesus. But everyone was so generous and welcoming that I tried to keep an open mind about my potential as a Christian. That said, none of the members of the youth camp caught my attention as much as a smoldering boy named Eric, who didn't seem to know any of the lyrics to the hymns we were singing, either. We made solid eye contact at least four times throughout the weekend, so I think it's pretty on point to say that he was in love with me. I decided that if he asked, I would 110 percent convert to Christianity for him.

When I came home from the weekend and told my parents I wanted to permanently join the youth group, my dad said I wasn't allowed. Before you criticize him for discouraging me from Christian theology, keep in mind that he and my mom had negative experiences with organized religion. Their decision to raise us as atheists was no different from another family's decision to raise their kids Christian or Jewish. Strangely enough, my religious friends were the ones who were either doing all the drugs or having all the sex in high school. Meanwhile, my uterus was lined with dust and cobwebs, and I was certain if I ever tried LSD or mushrooms, I would die from an instant heart attack. But according to my religious friends' strict beliefs, *I* was the one who would go straight to hell. I still struggle to see the logic in that.

So if this chapter had a thesis statement, it would be "SURPRISE! My parents are cool!" But I can't neglect the other 25 percent of that pie chart. Their views on sex and drugs are worthy of their own chapter, but there were a lot of other things we didn't agree on. Starting with:

— 1 —
My best friend's cleavage

Izzy McConnell wasn't one of my religious friends. She came from a family of bohemian hippies. At least they seemed bohemian compared to my parents. I loved Izzy's mom and dad and spent endless hours hanging out at their house. But I found Izzy's mom to be a contradiction in terms. I once heard her whisper to Izzy that I had left bread crumbs in her porcelain sink. She was notoriously compulsive about keeping their home spotless, and yet every nook and cranny of their house was filled to the brim with tightly organized clutter. (I'd never seen that many Beanie Babies in one place.) Izzy was not allowed to drink, under any circumstances, but Mrs. McConnell had no qualms about Izzy staying behind closed doors with her French-exchange-student boyfriend (a polar-opposite parenting style from my parents). She didn't allow Izzy to drive in cars with anyone who'd recently gotten their driver's license, but on the flip side (and unlike the rest of us), she was free to wear whatever she wanted. There was never a "no daughter of mine will leave the house looking like that" conversation in the McConnell home. Izzy was an incredibly talented artist and treated fashion like another form of self-expression. Since Izzy's mom never threw anything away, she'd kept every article of clothing she'd owned in the sixties and seventies. And since those decades were back in style during the nineties, we had a bevy of bell-bottoms, embroidered hippie tops, and flowing floral dresses to share between us. Some people thought Izzy dressed "weird," but I thought she was a trailblazer.

Izzy was also well endowed in the boob department and preferred to sport as much cleavage as possible without revealing areola. My parents definitely questioned why Izzy felt the urge to show so much boobage when their daughters never opted for low-cut tops. To be fair, I didn't have any cleavage. To be less fair, my sister did and she preferred turtlenecks, T-shirts, and flannels. I became so stressed out about Izzy's boobs that I would pray to a god I wasn't techni-cally supposed to believe in that she'd choose a less revealing top when she came over to my house. I know, I know, I know. It's not fair to judge a woman for owning her sexuality. We are not allowed as a society to criticize a person for topless selfies anymore. But back in the nineties, selfies didn't exist. We lived in a different world. A world where too much cleavage on a high school girl was still disarming. I was never embarrassed enough to ask Izzy to nix the cleavage when she was around my family, but when she did come over in her low-cut tops, it's possible that my parents started to wonder if Islamic law wasn't such a bad thing.

I don't think it was Izzy's boobs that were the problem. It was what her boobs represented. The fear that my nearest and dearest American friend might influence me in ways they didn't want me to be influenced. And they were right, because if it weren't for Izzy, I wouldn't have loved shopping at . . .

— 2 —
Thrift stores

My parents never openly discussed their money struggles, but I knew we didn't have disposable income. Our idea of a vacation was two days of car camping, or a night spent at the Napa Valley Embassy Suites so we could swim in their indoor pool. For most of high school, I had to go over to Izzy's house to type my papers, because we couldn't afford a computer. And yet my parents thought I was mentally incompetent for buying clothes at Goodwill. Why did I need used clothing when they were happy to give me a weekly allowance and when, thanks to finally having a Social Security number, I was making my own money? More important, why did I have an affinity for velour sweaters that resembled my dad's 1972 wardrobe and smelled like someone had taken their last breath in them?

"You don't get it," I'd tell them. "Grunge is in."

The only thing that disturbed my mom more than my clothing choices was my tendency to overaccessorize. Izzy loved rings and wore one on every finger, so I quickly did the same. Subtle and delicate was not the jewelry trend back then. Instead, we wore massive silver rings with brightly colored jewels and plenty of marcasite. The trend continued into college, and my mom's head nearly exploded when I went to an appointment at the Immigration and Naturalization Service (INS)* sporting my collection of sterling silver. I politely told my mom to pull it together. After years of living in the country illegally, I had a sneaking suspicion that my tacky taste in jewelry would not be grounds for deportation.

— 3 —
Bad manners

Iranians give the Brits a run for their money in the polite department. We're trained to give up our seats to anyone older than us, and to refer to our elders with titles of respect. We never talk back to our parents. There's like five hundred different ways to say "thank you" in the Farsi language. One

---

*In 2003, the INS was dissolved into three new entities: ICE, US Citizenship and Immigration Services (USCIS), and US Customs and Border Protection (CBP).

of our more common phrases is *"Daste shoma dard nakone,"* which literally translates to "May your hand not hurt." You generally say this when someone has cooked you a meal. The worst crime you could commit as a Persian human is to not have hot tea, pastries, cucumbers, nuts, and a basket of fruit at the ready when someone enters your house. Not to generalize, but being OCD about manners isn't exactly considered a quintessential American trait. And it wasn't for my high school social circle.

For starters, I had friends who didn't feel the need to say hello to my parents when they came over to my house. Perhaps they were intimidated by their foreignness, but I can still remember how my anxiety skyrocketed when my mom whispered to me in Farsi: "What's wrong with your friend? Is she mute? Why can't she even say hello?"

I had to train my friends to greet my parents the moment they saw them. There were also times I witnessed heated arguments between my friends and their moms that left me in a catatonic state. I couldn't believe anyone could get away with telling her mom to shut up. I was smart enough to know you were never meant to say such words out loud. You were meant to scribble them in a diary, hidden under the confines of a mattress. But there were moments when my parents reprimanded me, and I tried to defend myself by talking back. Big mistake. HUGE.

"You've been hanging out with your American friends too much," they'd say in their sternest of tones.

You might be thinking: "That's kind of racist." Or maybe

"really racist." But one of my parents' biggest fears after we immigrated to America was that we would abandon the most significant qualities of Iranian culture: our morals, our loyalty to and love for our family, our hospitality, and the lifelong desire to be kind and polite to others. At any sign that these virtues were slipping away, they began to panic that it had been wrong to bring us here. Maybe we would have been better off staying in Iran after all. If you're still not getting it, just picture what it would be like if you and your entire family abruptly moved to France. Let's pretend your parents were die-hard patriots. If you came home waxing poetic about socialism and ménages à trois, then they might be a little freaked out, too.

In the end, what I respected most about my parents was

My parents, circa 1996.

that when we didn't see eye to eye on certain topics, we were permitted to have a respectful dialogue. They had brought us to America for the sole reason of giving us a better life, and they didn't want that life to become an impediment to our relationship. The idea of their children growing up and no longer relating to them was a terrifying prospect. They knew the only way to avoid the inevitable cultural divide was conversation and compromise, even if it took a long and heated debate about the dangers of sterling silver jewelry to get to a place of mutual understanding. No topic was off-limits in our household. As much as their parenting philosophy was "We trust you," it was also "You can trust us."

September 15, 1996
I stayed home tonight and ate Chinese with my baba.
I love my family so much. They are extremely open-minded and easygoing. Me and Baba talked about things like boys and sex* for about an hour. We had the best conversation. I'm so thankful for my family. I'm so unbelievably lucky. It would be a blessing for me to grow up and become like my parents.

---

*I'm 99.9 percent sure the conversation with my dad about sex consisted of him telling me that it's the only thing guys want and that I can't fall for their crap.

FREQUENTLY ASKED QUESTION #2
What do Iranians have against Sally Field?

Sally Field is widely considered one of the best actresses of our time, but she's been persona non grata with Iranians after she starred in the overtly racist film Not Without My Daughter. It doesn't matter that the movie was released more than twenty-five years ago, because Iranians have a flair for holding lifelong grudges. The film painted Iranian Muslims, particularly Iranian men, in a very negative light. It pretty much made them all seem like abusive pricks. It was also released at a time when a Gulf war was brewing and when there were no other representations of Iranians in TV shows and movies. There still aren't very many representations, aside from the occasional terrorist character or the reality show Shahs of Sunset (also considered a form of terrorism to some).

In Not Without My Daughter, Sally Field plays an American woman trapped in Iran with a psycho husband who won't allow her to leave the country with their young daughter. The film was based on the popular and controversial memoir by Betty Mahmoody, and was critically panned for its racist depictions and Islamophobic tendencies. Though many compared it to a bad TV movie, it had lasting implications for Iranians. In the 2016 New York magazine article "The Not Without My Daughter Problem: How a Sally Field Movie Became an Iranian-American

Headache," writer Gazelle Emami talks to Iranian writer and scholar Reza Aslan on how the film affected his dating life:

"I am not joking when I say to you that at least on three separate occasions, when I met a girl's parents or immediately after I had met their parents, the girl would tell me how her mother brought up Not Without My Daughter . . . There was this one case in particular where on the second date the girl said, 'I can't really date you anymore. My mom doesn't want us to see each other.' I said, 'Why?' and she goes, 'Well, she saw that movie Not Without My Daughter.' I have numerous Iranian friends who have the exact same story—it ruined dating for every male Iranian of my generation."

For some reason (sexism), Alfred Molina, who played the abusive Iranian father, escaped our wrath.

Eventually, Sally Field earned back her goodwill with my family when she starred in the ABC drama Brothers & Sisters. My parents loved that show. They thought the Walker family was just like us . . . except for the fact that they were American, owned a swanky food-supply business in the quaint town of Ojai, and lived in a giant house in a very expensive Pasadena neighborhood. But those minor differences aside, my parents stand by the fact that we were basically the Iranian (and undocumented) version of Nora Walker and her dysfunctional brood.

I bought a book called Go Ask Alice. It's actually a teenager's diary. She's a really normal fifteen-year-old girl until she gets hooked on acid and pot. Toward the end of the book, she's getting her life together, after all the drugs, running away from home (twice), torment at school, and being in a mental hospital. There were a lot of things I could relate to about her. The whole diary thing connected me right away. Then, at the epilogue, they inform you that the "subject" of the book died three weeks later from a drug overdose. I'm gonna make all my friends read it.

—Diary entry: August 6, 1996

Chapter Five

✦ ★ ✦

Love and Other Drugs

"If you're going to do drugs, then bring them home and do them with me," my dad announced to me over a traditional breakfast of lavash bread, feta cheese, and sliced cucumbers. I nearly choked on my loghmeh.* It took me a minute to realize that he wasn't testing me. He was being serious.

"You got it, Baba," I said, knowing full well I never planned to try drugs with my dad.

"If anything happens to you, *I'll* know what to do," he continued. "Your friends won't."

This would not be a one-time offer. I would hear it so often during my teen years that I started to wonder if what he was really asking was for me to be his drug supplier. But

---

*Farsi for "finger food" or a small sandwich.

"Let's do drugs together!" was his leading parental philosophy on the subject of illegal substances, and it definitely fit into the "Super Cool" part of the pie chart. In an age where "Just Say No" and DARE were the prevailing antidrug campaigns, my foreign parents didn't have much faith that either would deter young people from getting high. They figured it was inevitable that one day, we kids would be pressured by our more rebellious peers to experiment with uppers and/or downers (there was no scenario where they thought *we* might be the ones doing the pressuring), and they preferred that we broadened our horizons with them, at home. It wasn't the drugs my parents were concerned with. They were more afraid of strung-out friends who might let us foam at the mouth and overdose to avoid getting in trouble with the authorities. My dad felt like it was better for us to experiment in a controlled and safe setting, and while his logic made sense to me, I never took him up on his offer.

At the start of high school, I was a total innocent when it came to substances like pot and acid and ecstasy. I knew that the slew of kids who hung out at Rainbow Park across the street from campus were considered our official brigade of stoners, but I'd never gotten high with them, and had no interest. Getting good grades and being accepted to a respectable four-year college topped my priority list. My focus on school was a side effect of battling stage-four ICGC, also known as immigrant child guilt complex. This is a chronic disorder that affects only children of immigrants, who experience a constant gnawing guilt for the multitude of sacrifices their parents made to bring them to the United States. There is no cure for ICGC, but treatments include making your mom and dad proud. (There is not a day that goes by that I don't look at my perfectly straight teeth—paid for by my parents—and think about the years of crooked teeth they've endured because they couldn't afford expensive dental work for themselves. This is why I always smile with my teeth showing in photos.) I knew as a teen that my parents had gone to great lengths to give me a better life, and killing my brain cells didn't seem like the most thoughtful way to return the favor. In short, I was a prude.

Even though my sister was one of the most popular girls in school, my friends and I didn't get invited to parties and had long decided we were too cool to attend any of our school events. We rolled our eyes at every high school convention that society tried to shove down our throats. Pep rallies: "LAME!" Football games: "NO ONE CARES!" School dances: "BOH-RING." I never admitted it to my friends, but I desperately wanted to participate in all of the above. From what I'd been told by John Mellencamp songs (listen to "Jack & Diane"), high school was supposed to be the best years of my life. I worried I was letting it pass me by. But while everyone else in our freshman class had gone to the same middle school and entered Lynbrook with their cliques already well established, my friend group and I were the unknown entities. We didn't mix well with the other kids and stuck together mostly by default.

As the school year ambled on, a few of us drifted away

from the group to hang out with the stoners at the park. I envied the girls who left us behind. I wanted to be less invisible. I wanted to hang out with the crowd of kids who went to parties on the weekends so they could get drunk and dry-hump in master bedrooms. But I didn't know how to ingratiate myself with the cool kids. Izzy claimed that drugs and alcohol were for losers and that we could have more fun hanging out in her bedroom and watching reruns of *The X-Files,* but I knew she was full of it. She wanted to go to parties as much as I did, but her mother was essentially holding her hostage in her house.

So for most of my freshman year, I remained a self-hating stick-in-the-mud. Even being in the presence of pot shined a light on how pathetically naive and innocent I was.

November 3, 1994
Today in music appreciation, Jonah asked me if I'd ever smoked pot, and I said "No, I bet I'm the only person in here who hasn't." So, he takes out his bag of pot and asks me if I like the smell, and I said how I really didn't think it smelled too good. So he passes it around and everyone's saying how they think it's the best smell in the world. I felt like such an idiot.

The above took place in what was essentially a storage closet where a small crew of us had been relegated to meet for a group assignment. It was four guys who were regular fixtures at Rainbow Park and me. I knew my aversion to the scent of marijuana meant I had blown my only chance at being cool. Why couldn't I have just pretended that I could roll a blunt with the best of them? More important, why did I care so much what a bunch of stoners thought of me? Well, for starters, it was an objective fact that the Jonah mentioned in my diary entry was one of the *hottest* guys in school. His smoldering brown eyes (which were always bloodshot) and his perfectly gelled brown hair bore a striking resemblance to those of a young Luke Perry (Archie's dad in *Riverdale*). But guys like Jonah who hung out at Rainbow Park didn't associate with the popular crowd. They were artsy misfits who dressed exclusively in concert tees and ragged flannels, and it was those brooding qualities that intrigued me more than the cookie-cutter athlete and cheerleader types. Even though I harbored a secret crush on Jonah, I knew at the tender age of fourteen that it wasn't wise to get wrapped up in someone with a drug problem. Little did I know that stoners would soon become my relationship kryptonite.

As the school year came to a close, I remained hopelessly drug-free. And I was becoming sick of my delicate state. I needed more edge. I wanted to know firsthand what all the fuss was about. Maybe there was nothing wrong with a little medicinal marijuana to treat my ICGC. Plus, if our application for a green card got denied, I wanted to revel in the perks of being an American teenager before the INS killed my vibe. It felt like smoking marijuana was my patriotic right. (Note: This rationalization lacked accuracy, because at the time, marijuana was, in fact, illegal in California. Which by definition meant it *wasn't* a patriotic right.)

It was a blistering hot summer afternoon in 1995 when I finally broke the vow I'd made to Nancy Reagan to just say no. A few days earlier, Samira had thrown herself a massive eighteenth birthday–slash–graduation party, and someone had left behind a backpack at our house, containing a bong and a bag of weed. I was swimming in our pool with Samira and our cousin Leyla when they came up with the brilliant idea to smoke me out.

"Let's get Sara high!" Samira announced.

Hallelujah, I thought. It was time to put my straitlaced ways to rest. I briefly considered my dad's offer: *If you're going to do drugs, then bring them home and do them with me.* Well, technically we *were* at home, and even though my dad was at work, doing drugs with my sister seemed like the next best thing. I knew she'd be able to handle it if anything went wrong. And anyway, everyone always told me that you don't get stoned your first time, so I expected smoking weed to feel comparable to smoking a cigarette (which I'd done before, thanks to my grandmother's nurse, who always kept a pack in her purse—I would sneak cigarettes from her and smoke in the bathroom when no one was home). Pot couldn't be that much different, right?

I listened carefully as my sister and Leyla gave me step-by-step instructions on how to take a bong hit. I followed their lead, and after two bong rips, I started laughing and couldn't stop. They giggled back at me, and declared to each other: "Sara's high!"

Finally, I had crossed the threshold. I thought of the girl who bristled at the smell of weed in music appreciation class and realized that I didn't want to be her anymore. I would go into my sophomore year of high school as the new-and-improved Sara. It didn't matter that my sister had graduated and I wouldn't be Little Sami. I didn't need to be. I could do anything!

And then I started feeling weird. Like, *really* weird. My forehead had developed its own giant pulse and it would not stop beating. I couldn't focus on anything. The heat was getting to me, and my mouth was so dry I couldn't swallow. My heart was racing, and there was only one thought going through my head: "I am going to die. I am going to die right now, and my parents are going to be *so* mad at me." Immigrant child guilt complex was bringing me down.

I gave my sister a panicked look and asked how long what I was feeling would last. She didn't have an answer.

"I don't like this," I said, tears streaming down my cheeks. "Get it to stop," I begged. But my sister and Leyla were too consumed by fits of laughter to help me. Where was my dad when I needed him? Maybe it would be a good idea to call him at work and let him know that I was about to die, and that I would miss him.

I walked into the house to get some relief from the heat, examine my face in the mirror, and call my dad to tell him I was mere moments from death. I barely recognized my reflection. My eyes were red and bleary. My little brother, Kia, was sitting on the couch, eating graham crackers and watching cartoons, and I desperately tried to act normal around him. What if he grew up to be a junkie, and when I caught him with a bent spoon under his thin dirty mattress, he'd scream that he learned how to do drugs from watching me? I sat on the couch to watch television and temporarily forgot about calling my dad, but the image of Scrooge McDuck swimming in a pile of gold coins did not improve my mental state, so I went back outside to avoid croaking in front of Kia. My eyesight was blurry and I could barely make out Samira and Leyla swimming in our pool. Their voices sounded muffled and distant. Was I going blind and deaf? Or was this what the world sounded like right before you died? I wasn't sure. Mostly, I didn't understand how my sister and cousin could function in their current state. If I jumped in the pool, I was certain I would forget how to float and sink to the bottom.

"Try to sleep it off," Samira advised, once she got out of the pool. In a couple of hours, our mom would be home from work, and we all knew it was critical that I started sobering up by then.

"Is this going to last forever?" I asked.

"No," my sister said, growing frustrated. "Relax. You're not even high!"

I know now that she was just trying to defuse the situation. If she could convince me that I was fine, then I would start to believe it. But her insistence that I was imagining my symptoms messed with my head even more. If this wasn't what being high felt like, then was there something else wrong with me? What if my brain had a different reaction to marijuana than other humans' brains had? Just great, I thought. I will never be able to take the SATs if I'm left in a permanent state of dumb. I tried to quiet the paranoia and curled up on a wet towel, spread out on the deck of our yard. I lay there, curled up in a ball, and attempted to fall asleep. But I thought if I closed my eyes, I'd probably never open them again. I was barely a teenager. This was so unfair. I didn't have a green card or a boyfriend yet. I had barely just gotten a work permit. How sad would it be to finally exist if I was just gonna die a few short months later? Thoughts of hot Jonah passed through my head, and I wondered how he managed to pay any attention in class with the world reverberating around him.

I could hear Leyla's and Samira's faraway voices as they tried to figure out what to do with drug-addled me. If my mom got home and found her daughter crying, eyes blood-shot, shouting to the heavens that she's "going to stay brain-damaged forever," she'd probably lose her shit and Samira would be grounded for the whole summer. They needed to fix me before that happened.

So they took me inside in hopes that getting some food in me might alleviate the steady heartbeat I was feeling in between my temples. I sat there quietly as they fed me Teddy Grahams and slices of watermelon. No fruit or box of pro-cessed food had ever tasted so good to me. I didn't feel like I was back to my normal self when my mom finally got home from work, but the fear that I was going to drop dead had gradually subsided. I tried to act sober around her, and she didn't seem to notice that anything was wrong. Eventually, the drugs wore off and I decided that I would *never,* under any circumstances, smoke pot again. It was a horrible drug. I didn't understand why anyone would ever want to feel so out of control. It was a terrible state of being. I much preferred to be alert and clearheaded.

But then I met Evan Parker and everything changed.

I warned you: stoners would become my kryptonite. I first noticed him that same summer when I spotted his school portrait in the yearbook. He was the only person in our four-hundred-plus freshman class I didn't recognize. How had I spent a whole year at Lynbrook without ever crossing paths with him? None of my friends knew who he was, either. When I showed up to school in the fall, he was in nearly all my classes. It was like the universe was trying to tell me something. I'm not entirely certain what drew me to stoner types like Evan and Jonah and the few others who came after them. I suppose they seemed more sensitive and introspective. They gave off major Jordan Catalano* vibes as they swaggered down the hallways of our school. It always felt like they had something better to do, and that unlike the rest of us, they understood that high school was an unnecessary social construct. Guys like them knew we could

*Played by Jared Leto in a seminal role, Jordan Catalano was the object of Claire Danes's character's affection in the cult-classic TV series *My So-Called Life.*

learn a whole lot more about life if we just paid attention to each other. In Evan's case, he also appreciated the little things, like ladybugs and lucky pennies and the clouds on a rainy day. He once gave me a poem he'd written titled "The Lonely Grasshopper," and I felt like he was showing me a window into his soul. He introduced me to musicians like Bob Dylan and Led Zeppelin. He could hacky-sack with the best of them, and knew how to skateboard. He was my ideal man.

I loved that he was deep and vulnerable and creative. These same qualities would cause me a lot of unnecessary heartbreak and grief in most of my adult relationships, but in high school, they set guys like Evan apart from the jocks and drama geeks. Evan also wasn't shy about extolling the virtues of weed and how it opened his mind to things he couldn't explore when he was sober. He also occasionally took drugs like acid and shrooms. I was way too afraid to explore either substance. If I had a panic attack from the most mild and natural illegal substance on the market, then it was safe to say I would experience a psychotic break on a hallucinogenic.

"If you think you're going to have a bad trip, you're going to have a bad trip," Evan warned me, and that was enough to prevent me from trying anything stronger than weed.

I loved Evan so much that when I visited Samira for a weekend in college and she took me to a hemp festival, I stocked up on hemp necklaces and hemp lip balm purely for his benefit. I knew the items would be the perfect conversation starter, and I wanted him to know I did cool things like hang out in college towns and go to hemp festivals.

My affection for him reached the point where he became my drug of choice. My highs and lows depended solely on how much attention he paid to me. And so when Evan asked me if I'd ever be interested in smoking out with him after school, I said: "Affirmative, love of my young life." Actually, I said: "Yeah, totally." I didn't tell him that I wasn't crazy about the way pot made me feel. As far as social lubricants went, I much preferred wine coolers and down-home punch. But mostly my vices included chocolate and pints of Ben & Jerry's.

A few days went by as I waited for Evan to make good on his invitation. When he did, I called my parents and told them I was staying late to help with the school play. I didn't feel an iota of guilt for lying. My heart nearly burst out of my chest as I spotted Evan waiting for me by the bus circle. He gave me a small wave as I made my approach, but my dreams were just as quickly dashed when he told me we were going to his friend Adam's house to smoke. I didn't want to hang out with Adam. I'd suspected in the past that Adam had a crush on me, and I was now left to wonder whether Evan's whole invitation was just a setup for me and Adam to hang out together. I was also hoping I would finally get to see the inside of Evan's house (especially since I'd covertly driven by it with friends multiple times, thanks to the stalking skills passed on to me by my sister). I wanted to know what his bedroom looked like. I wanted to know if he was messy or clean, and if he was nice to his mom when she was around, and if he arranged his CDs by any particular order. I wanted to know everything about him.

I didn't want to know anything about Adam. He was nice, but I wasn't attracted to him and found him far too clingy. I tried to be careful that anything I said to him didn't seem flirtatious, so that Evan wouldn't mistakenly think I was interested in his friend. So I barely spoke as we gathered in Adam's backyard and passed around a glass pipe. It was nothing short of a miracle that I managed to take several hits without coughing. But the romantic notions I had of the afternoon never materialized. After we finished smoking, we went inside the house and watched the movie *Friday* (where the phrase "Bye, Felicia" originated!). Evan sat on a recliner by himself, while Adam sat on the couch next to me. Even with my thoughts hazy, I could feel my heart sink as I stole glances at Evan. He was falling asleep. If he had any interest in me, he would have made more of an effort to make conversation. Or maybe he would have sat a little closer to me. When the time came and I had to leave, Evan was barely alert enough to say good-bye to me. I liked him much better when he was sober, I decided. I walked back to school alone and convinced myself I needed to do everything in my power to get over Evan Parker. A guy like him would never love me the way I deserved to be loved.

I was so consumed by my feelings for Evan that it never crossed my mind that smoking pot was a privilege afforded to American teenagers and not us undocumented kids. If

Evan got caught getting high, he could go to juvie. If *I* got caught, I'd have a criminal record that could be grounds for deportation. Maybe that was why my dad was so desperate to keep us from doing drugs with our friends. If my sister or I got arrested, it could cost all of us the ability to stay in the United States.

In spite of all this, my feelings for Evan only multiplied. I woke up one morning determined to spill my guts to him. If he knew how I felt, then maybe he would admit that he reciprocated my affections. I put on my cutest denim halter dress, straightened out my bob haircut, and wore a little more makeup than usual. When I got to school, I told Izzy that today was the day. I was going to confess my love to Evan Parker. And so, when I saw him in the distance, walking toward me during our twenty-minute brunch break, I stood up a little straighter and smiled a little wider. He smiled back.

This is it, I told myself. *The timing is perfect. Tell him how you feel.*

I'd practiced what I was going to say in my head a million times. I was going to tell him that I couldn't be his friend anymore, because I was in love with him. Evan walked over to me and gave me his usual bashful grin. He opened his mouth to speak, and these were the words that came out: "Can I have five dollars?"

I was speechless. In that moment, I realized that I'd been too generous with Evan and that he probably considered me the most likely sucker to give him a loan, because he already knew how I felt about him. I only got paid $5.65 an hour at my new job at Gap Kids. I wasn't about to give him an hour's worth of hard-earned money from folding pocket tees.

"No, sorry," I said at last. "I don't have any money."

The saga with Evan continued for a couple more years. There are two endings to our story, one where he irreversibly broke my heart, and one where he didn't. For now, I'll tell you the latter. It was a few weeks after graduation when we ran into each other at a party. I had a boyfriend at the time, but he would usually become an afterthought anytime Evan was in proximity. After some polite small talk, Evan told me that he was quitting pot and needed to find someone to bequeath his beloved pipe to. Of course, I offered to take it off his hands. He drove my car to his house, and I finally got to step inside the place where he spent most of his days. His bedroom was meticulously tidy. His shelves were filled with books on various religions. He talked to me about spirituality, and I pretended to be interested. And then he pulled a tiny canvas bag out of a drawer and handed it to me. Inside was his beautiful glass pipe.

July 21, 1998
Evan said he quit smoking pot, and I asked him what he was going to do with his pipe. He said he had to find someone to give it to. And I told him I wanted it . . . I let Evan drive my car to his house. I got to be in his house, in his room, sitting on his bed. And now I have his pipe. It was a dream. I could hardly sleep that

night. I just felt guilty. My feelings for him are real, and they've always been.

I don't have the pipe anymore. My parents confiscated it after little Kia found it in my bedroom and asked them why it smelled like cigarettes. Surprisingly, I did not get grounded. It's entirely possible my dad wasn't as offended that I was smoking pot as he was that I wasn't smoking it with him.

Mamani is here and she's driving all of us mad. I can't stand her. She's so selfish and awful. I'll be so happy when she leaves.

—Diary entry: August 27, 1999

Chapter Six

◆ ★ ◆

My Muslim Grandmother and Me

"Go back to your country" is one of my least favorite phrases in the English language. It's vile and racist and only uttered by xenophobes and bigots. And *yet* the words did run through my mind during the months or years that my dad's mom, Margaret Farideh Kanani-Ghasr, would come from Iran to live with us in America. Maman Farideh* (or Mamani, as we called her) regularly drove me nuts. I was mortified in movie theaters when my mom had to quietly translate every line of dialogue to her; I had no patience for her incessant nagging, or the fact that she couldn't seem to speak without spitting. The culture and generation gap that

_____

*When referring to your grandmother or grandfather in Farsi, you simply put the word "Maman" or "Baba" in front of their first name, but my grandmother primarily went by her middle name.

separated us was too immense to navigate. I was certain we were destined to never understand each other. Whenever I reached peak frustration levels, my parents liked to remind me that my grandmother had had a difficult life and that I needed to practice compassion. But that didn't make up for the fact that she was currently ruining my precious teen years. It never quite sank in that my life at fifteen was sunshine and roses compared to what she'd gone through as a teenager. Her existence was marked by a series of unthinkable losses. Mine was marked by aloof boys, prepping for the SATs, and a looming fear of deportation.

Mamani was born in France to an Iranian father and a Lebanese mother. She was the younger of two girls and adored her older sister. The two of them were completely inseparable until they were forced apart. They attended boarding school in France together (her whole life, she would remain fluent in French), but when Mamani was twelve, their mom passed away and their dad lost his job and decided to move the family to Tehran. He told his daughters they were merely going to Iran to visit family, so both girls mistakenly thought they'd be returning to their lives at school. But en route to Iran, their dad married off my grandmother's fourteen-year-old sister against her will. She didn't speak a word of Farsi and ended up married to an Iranian man who was in his early twenties. The sisters didn't know it at the time, but it would be ten years before they'd be reunited. My grandmother wrote her sister letters over the years, but as in every good tragic story, her sister never received them.

Three years later, my grandmother had her own arranged marriage, to a neighbor (my grandfather Mohammad Saedi) who was five years her senior. Everyone in my family called him Pedar Joon, which translates to "Father Dear."

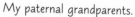

My paternal grandparents.

My grandmother moved in with him and his family, and at sixteen (when I was still yearning for my first kiss) she gave birth to my amoo* Abdullah (more commonly known as Abdol). My dad was born four years later, followed by my two aunts. My grandmother not only raised four children but also had a full-time job making clothing for Tehran's

---

*Amoo means "uncle on your dad's side" in Farsi.

elite class. While her employers were extravagantly wealthy, the Saedi family was considered lower middle class at best. But despite their lack of money, Farideh and Mohammad had a solid marriage. My grandfather was a kind and gentle man who made a very modest living working at a printing press. He wanted to protect his wife from his family's violent tendencies, but he couldn't exactly disown his parents. As a young boy, my dad regularly witnessed his mom getting beaten, and the image of her being abused remains burned into his memory. After one particularly violent incident, my seven-year-old dad took the bus to fetch his father at work so that he could hurry home and tend to my grandmother's bloody wounds. A year later, my grandmother would be so depressed by the harsh treatment she received from her in-laws that she tried to commit suicide by overdosing on opium. Luckily, she survived the suicide attempt, and by the time the kids were older, the in-laws were kicked out of the house and removed from their lives completely.

The Mamani I knew was incredibly independent and stubborn to a fault. She was also a strict Muslim. Whenever she lived with us in America, she would scramble to put on her head scarf if a male relative entered the house. She didn't drink alcohol or eat pork, and she always fasted during Ramadan. She made thirteen pilgrimages to Mecca, and faithfully prayed five times a day. I used to love peeking through doorways to her bedroom and watching her kneel on the floor and whisper "Allah Akbar." She seemed so focused and at peace during these moments of prayer and contemplation.

But when my dad was growing up, she preferred bright red lipstick to a chador.* He was often embarrassed to bring his friends around the house, because he didn't have a "typical" mom. Islam became a part of her life after the unexpected death of her oldest son, and religion became the only way she coped with the debilitating grief.

My amoo Abdol was handsome and charismatic, and taken from the world far too soon. At eighteen, he became one of the youngest soccer (or football, as it's more commonly known in Iran) players to join Team Melli, Iran's national team, and became a star in the country. His fame and income helped turn his family members' lives around. Thanks to Abdol's connections, my

My amoo Abdol at Amjadiyeh Stadium (currently known as Shahid Shiroudi Stadium).

dad was able to attend one of the best private schools in Tehran, free of charge. During and after his soccer career, Abdol was also a lieutenant in the air force. When he was thirty-one, he piloted a flight to northern Iran to pick up a high-ranking

---

*A chador is a large cloth that's draped around a woman's head and body, leaving only the face exposed.

official. The plane crashed on the way, killing my uncle and seven passengers. He left behind his wife and young daughter (my wonderful cousin Gita). My dad was in college in Baton Rouge when the crash occurred, and for two months, no one in his family told him that his brother, the person he loved most in the world, had perished. They were too afraid to break the news over the phone, and so they waited for his closest childhood friend to be able to tell him in person.

My grandmother was only forty-seven when her son passed away. Islam saved her life during this incredibly difficult period. Finding religion gave her a tiny bit of solace, and she remained a devout Muslim till the day she died. Six years after my uncle's death, my grandfather died of cancer. Mamani had gotten married at fifteen, became a widow at fifty-three, and spent the rest of her life on her own in an apartment in Mashhad, a city on the far eastern side of Iran. She came to America often and would live with us for long stretches of time. When I was a child, she drove me so crazy that I decided the only solution was to run away from home. I hopped on my bike barefoot and pedaled down the streets, determined never to return. I lasted about thirty minutes before returning home, kicking myself that I didn't take her advice to put on a sweater.

But there was one event in my life that connected Mamani and me forever: the time I broke my vagina. It was before puberty had fully arrived, so I didn't have much experience with blood and my private parts. My parents were away for the weekend, and my grandmother was in charge of watching us. I was making myself a snack in the kitchen, but due to the fact that I was vertically challenged, I couldn't reach a dish in one of our cabinets. I climbed up on the counter, as I often did to grab the dish, but when I hopped off, I didn't realize the door to the lower cabinet was ajar. I landed on it, with my legs wide open. I think it's safe to say if I were a boy, I would have died instantly from the pain. I thought for sure I would never bear children and that I'd need an emergency vaginoplasty. My grandmother found me screaming in agony, still straddling the cabinet door with my feet not reaching the ground. I was frozen. I was in so much pain, I couldn't move. I was crying, and she burst into tears when she saw me.

"Saaara! Saaara!" she screamed.

She slowly helped me off the cabinet door and proceeded to have a panic attack. She didn't speak any English and didn't have a driver's license, so she couldn't take me to the hospital. (In retrospect, she probably wasn't the best person to be taking care of us.) What if I bled to death from my vagina? How would she explain that to my parents? My own mental state became more fragile when I went to the bathroom and saw blood on my underpants. I was 99 percent certain I'd just lost my virginity to a cabinet door.

My grandmother immediately got on the phone with my khaleh* Shahrzad and explained the situation. My aunt rushed over and called my khaleh Mandana, who lived in

---

Khaleh means "aunt on your mom's side" in Farsi.

Los Angeles and worked as a nurse, for professional medical advice. My already humiliating day got worse when my khaleh Shahrzad announced that she'd been told to examine my vagina. I was horrified. I lay on my bed, completely mortified, as my aunt checked between my legs for any visible signs of trauma and permanent damage. Despite her lack of medical expertise, she said I looked fine. I wasn't totally convinced, but I was willing to agree, since the pain was starting to subside and there was no way in hell I was going to allow anyone else to look at my vagina ever again.

Despite the throbbing pain and humiliation, I'm grateful for my lady-parts injury. Though my grandmother and I didn't ever speak about it again, it was a terrible experience that bonded us. And for a woman who kept her emotions buried, seeing her in tears made me realize that she loved me. During her last visit to the States, we decided to take a walk together to a nearby Persian market. Long strolls were her favorite pastime, and that particular afternoon, the temperature was breezy enough to prevent her from getting too hot in her coat and head scarf. The streets in San Jose smelled like Maryam flowers, and as we walked the mile to the market, she pointed out other plants and foliage that she thought were beautiful. Even in her eighties, she would walk several miles each day at a brisk pace. In Mashhad, she walked everywhere. What I remember most about that afternoon was when she mentioned that in all her daily prayers, she always asked God to keep her two legs intact. She didn't see much reason for living if she couldn't be self-sufficient, and she couldn't be self-sufficient without her legs.

In 2011, she was hit by a car on one of her strolls in Iran. She was eighty-five years old, and while she survived the initial accident, she died from her injuries a few months later. The doctors said it was a miracle she survived at all, given her age, but that she was in incredible health for a person in her mid-eighties. I couldn't help thinking if she'd still been staying with us in California, the accident would have been avoided. I know she could have easily lived to be a hundred. I wish I had spent my adolescence less annoyed by and resentful of her presence. I wish I had made more of an effort to get to know her better. When a certain leader of the free world tried to impose a ban on Muslims entering the

Mamani in Santa Cruz, on her last visit to the States, in 2010.

country, I thought of my own family immigrating here, but I also thought a lot about Mamani. I know my parents had their reasons to raise us without religion, but it still upsets me to hear my grandmother's peaceful beliefs denigrated. She had a difficult life, but she didn't blame anyone. She was tough and knew how to take care of herself. But most of all, she was curious about the world and open to other people's belief systems. During that last stay in San Jose, she went on a walk, stumbled across a church service, and slipped inside. She couldn't understand what anyone was saying or doing, but she still wanted to observe and even dropped five dollars in the donation basket. I can imagine that some churchgoers may have been unsettled by this little old lady in a head scarf hanging out among a bunch of Christians. But I'd like to think they kept an open mind, like she always did, and that no one let the words "Go back to your country" enter their thoughts.

FREQUENTLY ASKED QUESTION #3
Why do Iranians keep watering cans in their bathrooms?

Well, this is embarrassing. If you've ever visited the home of an Iranian and noticed that they keep a watering can in their bathroom, it's not used to tend to our houseplants, though that was the lie I would tell my friends when they came over. Sometimes, I even went as far as hiding the watering can under the sink so that none of my friends would even see it. Here's the real truth:

We use them to clean our butts.

In European countries, most residential and hotel bathrooms come with bidets. The sole purpose of a bidet is to wash your ass, but they don't have them in America. I suppose Americans like to have dirty butts? Using our engineering prowess, we found a way to replicate the bidet by using a watering can to splash water on our asses. My uncle even travels with his. Now that I'm an adult with my own home, I decided to get in touch with my roots by purchasing my own watering can for my bathroom. Every time I look at it, I feel like a proud Iranian.

Tonight, Kia's kindergarten put on *Peter Pan*. Kia was Smee. He was so cute and good. I was so proud of him. Maybe one day, he'll be an actor . . . then I'll be so jealous.

—Diary entry: May 8, 1995

Chapter Seven

◆ ★ ◆

I Didn't Ask to Raise This Anchor Baby

Truth: my younger brother, Kia (named before the car became popular in the States), wasn't actually an anchor baby.* He was more like an accident. Fine, he was neither. If he had been an anchor baby, then my parents would have had him a lot sooner. Instead, they waited eight years after I was born to add another child to our family. Minus the fact that there had been no progress in our immigration status, my parents finally felt settled in the United States. They had their own business, a home, two daughters who could now speak English better than they could speak Farsi, and enough financial stability to afford another kid. Here's where President

---

*The term "anchor baby" refers to a child born to a noncitizen mother in a country that has birthright citizenship, especially when providing an advantage to family members seeking to secure citizenship or legal residency.

Donald Trump might tweet that they were financially stable because they were taking shortcuts and not paying taxes. For anyone who thinks that, let me assure you it's a bunch of malarkey. My parents received Social Security numbers and work authorizations when they lived in Louisiana during my dad's college years in the seventies (before the hostage crisis and back when they handed those puppies out like lollipops at a rave). They paid taxes just like everyone else and paid for private health insurance for our family. They were also able to own a business and eventually buy a home (and pay property taxes), which paved the way for a bundle of joy.

Little eight-year-old me cried tears of happiness when I learned my mom was pregnant and I was going to have a little brother. It didn't quite click that getting a new sibling meant I would give up my coveted spot as the baby of the family. Instead, I would be demoted to middle child. Otherwise known as the forgotten kid. But even without my downgrade in the birth order, Kia was a huge disappointment once he entered the world. When Samira and I arrived at the hospital to meet him, he'd taken a wet poop in his diaper, and his belly button looked like a giant, grotesque scab. The wails and screams that escaped from his tiny mouth sounded like those of a dying litter of meerkats. The hospital room smelled like shit and regret. My sister was so disturbed by the whole thing that she puked her guts out.

Gradually, natural selection kicked in. Kia got cuter, and I decided he could live. My parents like to claim that after he was born, I frequently locked myself in the bathroom and very loudly plotted schemes to run away from home, because no one paid attention to me. But I don't believe their lies. The way I remember it, I was quickly obsessed with Kia.

During his daytime naps, I'd wait for my mom to take a shower, and then I'd carefully scoop him out of his crib so I could cradle him in my arms. He was so light and precious, and since I had eight years on him, I already felt like he was my responsibility. But no one told me that as the years went on, I'd actually be in charge of raising him. I would be a teen mom and a virgin. Arguably, the world's most depressing combination.

By the time Kia turned seven, he and I were the only ones left in the house. Samira was off at college, and my parents worked long hours to keep their struggling luggage business afloat. It was on me to pick Kia up from school and walk him home. We'd arrive to an empty house, and I'd make him a snack and force him to watch *Days of Our Lives* or *The Oprah Winfrey Show* with me. He was a regular fixture in my life. If friends wanted to hang out after school, it was always with the understanding that my little brother would tag along.

Back when you didn't know how a selfie would turn out. We were so brave.

When I worked at Baskin-Robbins, he'd occupy a booth and do his homework during my four-hour shifts. When I got a higher-paying job at Gap Kids, he'd hang out at the mall, try on the latest in children's fashions, and eat his way through the food court. Toward the end of high school, I landed a barista gig at a popular local café, and Kia came to work with me almost daily. I supplied him with coloring books and bottomless hot chocolates. And I also forced him to wipe down the tables and help me mop. The kid was better than cheap labor. He was *free* labor.

In many ways, Kia was the outlier of our family. He was the only boy, and far younger than my sister and me. He didn't have to lose sleep over getting deported. He became an American citizen simply by being born in the United States. That, my friends, is a shortcut. But if our application for permanent residency got denied by the government and we were shipped back to Iran, then Kia's citizenship status wouldn't make a difference. There was no way we would leave him behind. He would have to come with us. His ability to live in the United States depended on our ability to live here. But that didn't change the fact that he never had to put up with long lines at the INS, mountains of paperwork, and a baseline fear that we could get escorted out of the country at any moment. Even though he was only in second grade, he was technically free to backpack through Europe, or go on safari in Africa, and breeze through customs upon his return. He was eligible to run for president of the United States . . . though he'd probably have a better chance of getting elected if he'd been raised by a pack of wolves than a pack of illegal immigrants. Most of all, he didn't have to go to any humiliating lengths to get a green card like I did.

If you want to see a teenage illegal immigrant's already fragile self-esteem hit rock bottom, just take them to get their passport photo at a location where they might run into someone from high school. This wasn't just any passport photo. It was a picture to renew my Iranian passport. Post-revolution, Iran had issued a new form of birth certificates, and we needed to secure replacements. In order to make that happen, I needed to send an updated passport photo to the Interests Section of the Islamic Republic of Iran, which was housed in the Pakistani embassy in Washington, DC. Those details aren't important. What really matters about this story is that I had to sport a head scarf in the photo. I was filled with anxiety as my mom drove Kia and me to our local Photo Drive-Up. The store doesn't exist anymore, but back in the nineties, you could go there to develop photos *and* rent movies—two activities that are obsolete today, hence its disappearance. I don't know why Photo Drive-Up enjoyed torturing their customers, but they made you take your passport photo out in the open—so that anyone perusing the new-releases aisle could watch. Since my parents didn't raise us Muslim, this was the first and only time I ever had to wear a scarf to cover my hair. I didn't have anything against people who chose to wear a head scarf. It was a perfectly good solution to a frizzy-hair day. Plus, I'd grown accustomed to the eclectic collection of scarves Mamani used to cover up her gray curls. But my hair was one of my most acceptable features. It distracted people from my large nose and the signature Persian dark circles under my eyes.

Maybe if I weren't an atheist, God wouldn't have punished me by having one of the most popular girls in school walk into Photo Drive-Up at the very moment my picture was being taken. My heart nearly stopped from the public humiliation once she spotted me. I suddenly felt exposed.

My passport photo. (Fun fact: September 21, 1980, is not actually my real birthday. I'll explain later.)

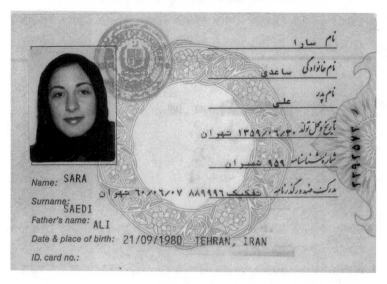

Name: SARA
Surname: SAEDI
Father's name: ALI
Date & place of birth: 21/09/1980 TEHRAN, IRAN
ID. card no.:

Today, the photo no longer embarrasses me the way it did when I was a teenager. Sure, it's not the most flattering image, and I wish I'd never gone through a dark-lip-liner phase, but there's absolutely no reason to be embarrassed for sporting a head scarf. Muslims also had it somewhat easier back then. My grandmother never got harassed when she walked around our neighborhood in her head scarf during the mid-nineties. There had been enough distance from the hostage crisis of the seventies, and the Gulf War of the early nineties. September 11 hadn't happened yet, and we were decades away from living in Trump's America. The Muslims I knew didn't have to be afraid to be seen in public wearing the hijab the way they are today. If I had to do it all over again, I would have proudly ignored the confused glances from the popular girl from school, but in the moment, the only thing that got me through the photo shoot was Kia standing on the periphery, giggling at me. He was so amused by my new look that it was almost impossible not to find the humor in the situation. Which only irritated the photographer and made the shoot take even longer, since I wasn't supposed to smile in the picture.

Most days, I didn't resent the fact that my brother spent a lot of time in my care. My parents didn't want to be absent, but they weren't left with much choice. They had a mortgage to pay, on top of college tuition for my sister, and that meant working overtime. Our setup was typical of most immigrant families: the mom and dad tried to make ends meet, while the kids took care of each other. And even with their busy work schedules, my dad was still able to find time to coach Kia's soccer team, and my mom still chaperoned Kia's school field trips and attended all his games.

But as long as I was in charge of "raising" Kia, I decided I would also mold him into the world's most sensitive boy. I didn't want him to be self-involved and distant like the stoner boys I pined for in high school. If it were up to me, Teen Kia would treat girls with love and respect. He would be a stand-up guy. He wouldn't string anyone along. And that's why every time I was faced with yet another setback in my romantic life, I'd purposely break down in tears in front of Kia. I'd make him pinkie-swear that he wouldn't grow up to be an asshole. I thought if he witnessed my rocky mental state, he'd come away with a unique understanding of the female psyche and would tread carefully with other people's hearts. It probably just made him think women were certifiable.

I may have gone a little too far in the parenting department here. By second grade, Kia was a hopeless romantic. When I picked him up from school, his mood was dependent on how much time he'd spent with his grade school crush. If they flirted during recess, then life was good. If she paid attention to one of his friends instead, he was devastated. I tried to tell him that he was young and that there were a lot of fish in the sea, but it was little consolation. Thanks to me, even in adulthood, Kia has been known to call me in tears over a girl or a breakup. I didn't tell him this, but there's a good chance he suffered from PTSD from all the times I forced him to watch me sob over a boy while listening to the song "Foolish Games" by Jewel* over and over again.

If my sister was more guarded with secrets until I got older, then I was an open book with Kia. He hadn't even reached double digits yet, and he had a detailed account of every high school boy I loved. He knew which girl from my clique I was

*Jewel was a formerly homeless folk singer who gained popularity in the nineties. Her "Foolish Games" spoke to me on so many levels. It felt like it had been written about Evan Parker and me.

most closely aligned with, and which girl was currently in friendship purgatory. But trusting him with the classified details of my heart turned out to be a rookie mistake. At fifteen, there were few things worse than your crush's identity being revealed to the rest of the school. My girlfriends and I were very sly at keeping the objects of our affections on the down low. We never wrote their names in notes, in case the notes fell into the wrong hands. We resorted to secret code names like Wallace (for the boy who was obsessed with the movie *Braveheart* and William Wallace) and Checkers (for the boy who wore checkered Vans) whenever we discussed any of them aloud. And we made it abundantly clear that if any of us squealed to members outside of our inner circle, it would be a friendship ender.

Kia knew all about my love for Evan Parker (code name: Samson, for his long hair). Even my parents knew about Evan. I talked about him nonstop. I had no interest in other guys at school. He was the only person for me. But even though we never dated, our friendship was wrought with conflict. Whether Evan knew it or not, he hurt me on a daily basis by dating other girls or referring to me by unflattering nicknames. One day his gorgeous Asian girlfriend pointed out in Spanish class that I was the spitting image of Anne Frank, and he enthusiastically agreed. Don't get me wrong: Anne Frank was a hero. Her diary entries were far more profound than mine, and bravely put a face to the millions killed in the Holocaust. But I still knew that when you referred to a girl as Anne Frank, it probably didn't mean you wanted to get into her pants.

Either way, aside from the few lapses in sanity when I considered revealing my true feelings to Evan, I was mostly desperate to keep my love for him under wraps. I was terrified that if he knew how I felt about him and didn't reciprocate my feelings, then we'd cease to be friends. My besties guarded my secret feelings with their lives, but it was my little brother who accidentally let the cat out of the bag. School was done for the day, but I'd brought Kia back to campus so I could hang out with Izzy. We ran into a boy named Ben, who happened to be one of Evan's best friends. I had hoped cozying up to Ben would give me some indication as to whether Evan had any interest in me, but Ben wasn't exactly the most verbal of boys. He mostly talked about his love for playing the drums and why Neil Peart was a rock god. I never brought up Evan on my own, because I worried it would be obvious that I liked him as more than a friend. But since Kia had witnessed a bevy of my mental collapses, he considered Evan a raw wound. He was trying to be a supportive younger brother, but he totally blew up my spot instead.

It happened so fast that I didn't even see it coming. Ben mentioned Evan's name, and before I had time to react, Kia piped in with:

"How *dare you* mention that name in front of my sister?"

It was my fault. If I hadn't made him watch so many episodes of *Days of Our Lives,* he wouldn't have developed a nasty habit of speaking in the vernacular of a soap opera villain. I was caught. I was mortified. It was obvious by Kia's melodramatic tone that the Evan topic was off-limits because I was (a) madly in love with him and (b) deeply scarred by him. Ben tried to gracefully change the subject, but we both knew I'd been exposed. In that moment, I would have done anything for a customs agent to appear and drag me away to the airport. I would have gladly packed my bags and moved back to Iran just so I would never have to see Evan or Ben or Kia ever again.

Izzy and I let Kia have it once we left Ben and got in my car. I screamed at him so loud that he started to cry and mumbled apologies as his chin trembled. But I wouldn't stop. In that moment, any deep-rooted resentment I had for being trailed my whole life by my younger brother came to the surface. Why did I have to take care of him? Why did both my parents have to work? Why did they even need to have another kid in the first place? I didn't speak to Kia for days. Everything seemed status quo at school, so I never found out if news of the awkward exchange reached Evan. Eventually, I forgave Kia for his mistake and apologized for yelling at him, and returned to my favorite hobby: lying in bed and listening to depressing songs that perfectly captured my longing and despair. My all-time favorite was "It Ain't Me Babe" by Bob Dylan. I'd often close my eyes and pretend that Evan was the one singing to me.

I would still have Evan Parker on my mind the night before I left home for college. I'd begged my dad to take Kia and me to a Bob Dylan concert, even though the venue was a long trek from our hometown. It was cold and windy that night, but we bundled up in a blanket on the arena's lawn as we listened to Dylan's gravelly voice. It didn't sound the same as all the CDs I'd been listening to. Kia was probably the youngest person at the concert, but I wanted my last night with my brother and parents to be memorable. We left the show worn-out and weary, knowing that the next day I would be gone and Kia would go from being the baby of the family to an only child. The University of California, Santa Cruz, was merely a forty-five-minute drive on the curvy roads of Highway 17. Izzy and our other best friend, Paige, had also enrolled at UCSC, so I took some comfort in knowing I wouldn't be surrounded by strangers. The close drive would make it easy to see my family on the weekends, and I promised Kia he could come visit whenever he wanted. I already knew I'd had a hand in turning him into a sensitive kid, but I never expected him to go into an ugly cry when we said good-bye outside the dorms. Only three years before, I'd broken down when we took Samira to college. I knew Kia and I had a close bond, but I never realized quite what I meant to him until that moment. He wasn't just losing his sister; he was losing his surrogate mom. He would come to visit a bunch of times, which made him the only ten-year-old who showered and brushed his teeth in our dorm's coed bathrooms.

It's possible my parents hadn't been lying. Maybe I did spend hours in the bathroom after Kia was born, fists clenched, shouting to the heavens that I'd been dealt a crappy hand. But it turned out the notion that being a middle kid was a form of child abuse was greatly exaggerated. In my experience, being the middle child meant straddling the best of both worlds. I got to experience what it was like to have an older sibling take care of me, and I also got to experience what it was like to take care of someone else. Years later, after I'd settled in Los Angeles, Kia enrolled as an undergrad at UCLA, and we picked up where we left off. With me as the worried mother figure who consoled him over bad breakups, and him as the sensitive kid who listened and supported me through my meltdowns. All my plans for him had come to fruition: he'd grown up to be a stand-up guy. My job was finally done. At last, I had proof that I'd raised him well. But that shouldn't have come as a surprise to me. I recently stumbled upon a card I wrote to him for his eighth-grade graduation and was reminded that, even at thirteen years old, Kia was on track to becoming a good person. Here's an excerpt:

> I'm so incredibly proud of you. I can't tell you what it felt like to drive you to school in your cap and gown—and to see how many kids obviously love you at that school . . . I remember it like it was yesterday when I took you to orientation. I was so nervous for you then—going to a school where you didn't know anyone. But look how many friends you made, how involved you got, and with straight A's too!

See. I told you. Surrogate mom for the win.

I'm really fed up with people right now. I got my eyebrows done, and the lady was telling me if I ate two lemons a day, I wouldn't get zits. It's like telling a fat person about this new diet when you're really skinny. When I look in the mirror, I agonize about my skin. I think about it constantly, only to hear my parents lecture me on how if I ate better food, I'd have no zits. It's not that easy. They never had bad skin. They wouldn't know. Screw them. If they ever read my diary, this entry will tell them how their comments are eating me up inside, probably causing more zits.

—Diary entry: August 29, 1996

Chapter Eight

◆ ★ ◆

Rhinoplasty Acne-pocalypse

"There's something we need to talk about." My mom said the words in a tone most would reserve for a cancer diagnosis.

"Okay . . . ," I replied.

My stomach plummeted as she slowly approached my bed and sat next to me, subtly avoiding eye contact. It was evident from her cagey behavior that, whatever the topic, this conversation would not end well. Which left me with one option: jump out of my second-floor bedroom window. Before I could appropriately measure whether risking death or a spinal injury was a worse fate than an uncomfortable mother-daughter exchange, she dropped this bomb:

"I've been thinking about it, and I want you to go on birth control."

What. The. Hell?

A conversation about prescription contraceptives was not what I'd expected. At least now I had solid proof that my mom wasn't reading my diary. If she had been perusing my cursive hopes and fears, she would have known I was a seventeen-year-old virgin who was still fumbling around with masturbation. What made her think that I was going to have sex? None of my friends were on the pill. Not even the ones who were sexually active.

"Um, I'm not having sex," I admitted.

"Oh, I know that," she said, a little too quickly. "But your khaleh Mandana told me that going on the pill might help clear up your skin. Do you want to try it?"

At what was a very sensitive juncture in my life, my mom could have told me that cutting off my legs would help clear up my acne, and I would have gladly become a double amputee. For years, my formerly clear skin had been under the occupation of the People's Republic of Pimples, and I'd done everything to reclaim its independence. I'd tried every over-the-counter zit medication known to man, along with harsher prescription creams like Retin-A or pills like erythromycin that were recommended by my dermatologist. I tortured myself by not eating chocolate for months, hoping that a change in diet would rid my face of pimples. I washed my face three times a day. When the Proactiv infomercials hit the airwaves, my mom paid for a rush order, but even the face wash, toner, and lotion combo couldn't conquer my clogged pores and whiteheads. Izzy and Paige were also victims of bad skin. We tried facials and mud masks at every sleepover, and took great joy in photographing ourselves covered in zit medicine.

But of the three of us, I suffered from the worst kind of pimples. The kind doctors refer to as hormonal cystic acne. These are the zits you can feel for days before they fully emerge on your skin in all their glory. And when they do, they're usually as large as a marble. They're painful and take months to heal. I tried my best to resist the urge to pop my zits, because I'd been warned that would cause scarring, but they never seemed to go away on their own. I felt like I was in a no-win situation, but the battle would have been much harder to wage if I hadn't had my closest girlfriends in the trenches with me. It helped to have allies in the fight on our sebaceous glands. We could trade war stories about our latest dermatologist visits and new favorite products. Izzy taught us how to hide our zits with foundation and concealer. Eventually, Paige decided to bite the bullet and go on Accutane, a new acne pill on the market that came with harsh side effects. Paige was on a high dose, and during her shift working at a gourmet grocery store, she started bleeding from her eyes and nose. Her co-workers called an ambulance and she was rushed to the hospital. The experience left her shaken and embarrassed, *but* her skin eventually cleared up. Silver lining! I was jealous of Paige's courage. I didn't think I could handle the risk of bleeding out of every orifice in public, even if it meant no longer cursing my reflection.

For the most part, I'd been a late bloomer. I got my period after most of my friends, and wore a training bra before I had boobs to support. But I was *eleven* when I got my first zit. It was in sixth grade (back when I was cool), and it made a cozy home for itself on my chin. I had enough natural confidence to know the best way to survive my new facial deformity was to own it like a boss. I named the pimple Peter and lamented to everyone who would listen about Peter's poor timing, with picture day just around the corner. I didn't realize that Peter marked the beginning of the end. My skin would never be the same again. By middle school, I lost the will to be charming and self-deprecating about my faulty pores. It was in eighth grade when I got a painful and prominent red zit on my forehead. I tried to wear a backward baseball cap to cover it up, but everyone knew of its existence. I remember sitting on a bus on the way back from a field trip when a boy from my class shouted, "Hey, Sara! Do you worship Gandhi?"

Get it? Cause the red zit reminded him of a bindi. I wish I'd had more of a backbone then. I wish I'd shouted back that I did worship Gandhi, because he was a powerful historical figure who helped free India from British rule. I could have yelled back that the Hindu culture was beautiful and that samosas were freaking delicious. But instead, I burst into tears.

"You're so sensitive," the boy said to me.

"You're so *in*sensitive" was the best comeback I could muster.

When I got home, I crawled into bed and wept like a baby. My mom tried to console me, but there wasn't much she could say to make me feel better. No one else in my family had bad skin. Aside from the occasional pimple, my sister had a perfect complexion. And my brother was far too young to deal with zits (spoiler alert: even puberty didn't disrupt his skin). Breakouts weren't a staple genetic flaw for Iranians. We were used to imperfections we could fix with plastic surgery or painful hair removal. And that's why my parents were convinced that it was my proclivity for sweets and aversion to vegetables that caused my acne. When my mom finally learned that hormones were involved, she decided it would be worth putting me on birth control.

The pill was by far my favorite acne treatment. I felt cool telling my friends that I was taking oral contraceptives. I loved the plastic container the monthly dose of Ortho Tri-Cyclen came in, and that I could keep track of the day of the week by using the turnstile to pop my next fix of estrogen. Even though I wasn't having sex, I was religious about taking each dose at the same exact time every day, like the instructions suggested. It didn't matter if my clitoris continued to elude me, I felt like a grown woman. I didn't even care that the first few pills of the month would make me so queasy that I had to bolt out of class and vomit in the bathroom. I was a badass. The extra estrogen did help clear my skin some, but not to the extent that my mom and I were hoping.

My traumatic experiences with bad skin happened before terms like "fat shaming" and "slut shaming" were invented, but even today, no one seems to mention that skin shaming also exists. Most people had the sense not to share a dieting trick with an overweight person, but no one seemed to think it was wrong to share their acne remedies with me. I had more than a few unsavory experiences with peers and adults who were quick to point out my problematic skin. For starters, there was the time a buxom blond cheerleader with flawless skin and adorable freckles very loudly declared in science class that students with acne should "just wash their faces."

It didn't matter if I scrubbed my face daily. I knew that the kids with perfect skin were just as blessed as the ones who were naturally thin.

And then there was the Persian eyebrow threader who decided to dole out skin advice while she kept my evil unibrow at bay. Threading hurt like a mother, and my eyes always watered from the unbearable pain. But on the day my eyebrow threader suggested that if I ate two lemons every day I'd get rid of my zits, the tears that filled my eyes weren't just from the agony of tiny hairs being pulled out by the root. I did try to eat two lemons a day, but it didn't work. Fine, maybe I only tried it one time, but I'm still convinced it's an old Persian wives' tale.

But the worst was the time a total stranger commented on my skin. I had pulled into the parking lot of our local pharmacy to run an errand, and checked my skin in the rearview mirror like I often did before getting out of the car.

"Yes!" I thought to myself. "I'm having a good skin day!"

I picked out everything I needed at the store, and stood in line at the checkout. A girl who used to live down the block from me was manning the register. I'd always felt bad for her, because she was on the heavier side, and I imagined that wasn't an easy way to go through high school. An elderly woman was in line in front of me. She turned to me, smiled broadly, and then said, "My grandson has a lot of zits. I can see that's something you have experience with. Do you have any advice for him?"

First of all, why ask someone with bad skin to give advice to someone else with bad skin? That's the equivalent of asking someone with a beer gut for tips on how to get a defined six-pack.

"Tell him to go on birth control," I should have said, but didn't. Instead, I recommended he see a dermatologist.

The girl at the register looked at me with an expression of utter and genuine sympathy that I'd never seen on another human being before, and quietly whispered, "I'm so sorry."

"It's okay," I managed to say, but I felt like someone had reached into my chest, pulled out my heart, and dropped it in a meat grinder. If I was getting comments about my acne on a *good* skin day, then I was monumentally screwed.

By college, I finally decided to give Accutane a shot, but it took two rounds to alleviate most of my skin problems. The medication was aggressive, and I was required to stay on oral contraceptives and to get a blood test every month to prove that I wasn't pregnant before they prescribed me the next round of pills, since one of the side effects of the drug was severe birth defects. I hated the fact that Accutane made my eyes look perpetually red and my lips feel perpetually chapped, but in the end, it was worth it (for me). I still didn't achieve perfect skin. Some of my acne scars never went away, but I was much better off than I'd been without it. And luckily, no one had told me yet that adult acne was a real thing. Accutane was discontinued in 2009, though generic versions remain on the market. While Roche, the manufacturer, claimed they discontinued the drug due to the patent expiring, some believe it was the bevy of lawsuits linked to the medication. Aside from severe birth defects, it was also linked to depression, suicidal tendencies, and bowel disorders. It's probably the most hard-core drug I've ever done.

At least my battle with bad skin felt like a disorder I could somewhat control, but there were no over-the-counter creams or prescription pills that could decrease the size of my famously large Persian nose. For years, my parents and relatives tried to convince me that I'd been blessed with a normal-size nose. I would come to realize that this was a flat-out lie. It was true that the bridge of my nose didn't come with a hump, but it was still long and bulbous. In profile, my nose jutted way past my chin and upstaged the rest of my features. It quickly became my archnemesis (no pun intended).

My sister hated her nose, too—hers was smaller but more rotund than mine—and my parents agreed that something needed to be done about it. And so, for her seventeenth birthday, they offered to get her a nose job. I was stunned. She'd barely been allowed to pluck her eyebrows, but they didn't think seventeen was too young for major plastic surgery? But I also knew that Samira (whom I considered gorgeous) was very self-conscious of her nose. If changing it would really make her feel better about herself, then who was I to stand in her way? I would have preferred that the money go toward a desktop computer, but I decided to keep my mouth shut.

Nose jobs are a common practice among Iranians. My mom got one soon after she married my dad. Most of my female cousins have gotten them, too. So during the summer before her senior year of high school, my parents sent my sister off to Los Angeles—otherwise known as the plastic surgery mecca of the world. There was an Iranian doctor in Beverly Hills who'd come highly recommended, and he'd agreed to give my parents a good deal. Samira would stay with family in Southern California while she recovered from the procedure. A few days later, we went to the San Jose airport to pick up my sister and to see her new nose for the first time. I was nervous. What if the transformation was so extreme that I wouldn't recognize her? When she walked out of the terminal, her face was bruised and swollen. For the most part, she looked like the same person. Her nose didn't necessarily seem better to me, just different. But the surgery did wonders for her self-esteem. She hated her nose so much that she didn't even wait until college to have the procedure done. She was willing to risk the awkwardness of arriving to school her senior year with a brand-new facial feature. In my opinion, that was just further proof that Sami Saedi was a force to be reckoned with.

After my sister's procedure, my parents continued to insist that I didn't need a nose job. My friends also convinced me that my current nose was just fine. They even threatened to stop talking to me if I got plastic surgery.

"You'll look like a different person," Izzy and Paige would say.

I've already mentioned my ravishing mom. Sometimes my aunts and uncles would look at me and gently slap their cheeks, awestruck by the fact that I looked just like her.

"It's like looking at a young Shohreh," they would say.

I didn't see it. My poor middle-aged relatives probably had cataracts. My mom and I didn't resemble each other at all. But then I stumbled upon old photographs of her in Iran, pre–nose job.

"Holy shitballs . . . ," I thought. It felt like I was looking in a mirror. She had my nose. She'd always claimed her old nose was much bigger than mine, but I didn't see any difference between them. How could my mom tell me I was pretty when she'd looked just like me and had gone through plastic surgery to change her face? What harm would it do if I jumped on the plastic surgery bandwagon? I had aunts who'd gotten face-lifts and even a cousin who'd gotten her ears pinned back. If I joined the club, no one in my family would pass judgment. Back in Iran, nose jobs were a sign of wealth and privilege. Some people liked to walk around the city with bandages across the bridge of their noses, just so people would think they'd gotten surgery. So what was stopping me?

Fear. Fear that even if it made me look prettier, it would also make me look *different*. Even worse, what if I liked my old face better than my new face? Getting rhinoplasty wasn't the same as getting a haircut. Your old nose wouldn't grow back if you hated the new one. I told myself that I didn't have to follow the plastic surgery trend that had taken my family by storm. (Plus, I don't think my parents could have afforded *two* nose jobs for their kids.) Instead, I would embrace my big nose. Just as Beyoncé sings in her song "Formation," "I like my Negro nose with Jackson Five nostrils," I would like my Persian nose with Barbra Streisand nostrils. Yeah, I know Streisand isn't Persian, but it's the best pop culture example I could come up with.

In all honesty, I still hate my nose. There are traits I was self-conscious about in my teen years that I've come to

My mom at eighteen.

Me at eighteen.

embrace in adulthood (my height, my big booty, and my curly hair, for example), but my nose never managed to win me over. When a doctor told me that I had a really bad deviated septum, it seemed like a good excuse to go under the knife. But I never did, and I probably never will. There's enough about me that doesn't look Iranian. Almost every Persian person I meet is surprised when I whip out my broken Farsi. Even my name gets bastardized all the time (the *ar* in Sara rhymes with "car," not "care"). But my nose is undeniably Persian, and changing it would feel like rejecting the most significant part of myself.

FREQUENTLY ASKED QUESTION #4
What is the deal with Iranian weddings?

There is no single event for Iranians that has more significance than a wedding. The guest list alone can ruin lives, destroy families, and create deep wounds that take years to heal. This is generally why Iranian weddings are so big. It's not because we have an array of relatives we can't imagine not having present on our big day. It's because we are terrified of offending anyone by leaving them off the invite list. I've personally witnessed several family rifts because so-and-so didn't invite so-and-so to their wedding even though they had the nerve to invite a family friend. If you're Persian and you want to cut someone out of your life forever, there's a really easy way to do it: don't invite them to your wedding or your kid's wedding or your grandkid's wedding. I guarantee they will never speak to you again, and after you've died, they will visit your grave only to pee on it.

I can't provide factual evidence as to why weddings became such an integral part of the Iranian culture. In modern-day Iran, men and women aren't technically allowed to celebrate in the same room together, but many are willing to break the law to cut a rug. The Iranian culture doesn't have any ceremonies that recognize rites of passage like quinceañeras or bar mitzvahs (unless of course you are a Persian Jew, which we aren't), so weddings became our only opportunity to get dolled up, attend a big party, and dance to Iranian hits with the occasional Gipsy Kings tune thrown onto the playlist. Unlike most American weddings I've attended, Iranian weddings call for formal clothing—it's a cardinal sin to show up wearing a summer dress or something perfectly appropriate for a Sunday church service. We take wedding attire as seriously as Anna Wintour takes the Met Gala. We are strictly black-tie. In fact, the only reason an Iranian wedding would be "black tie optional" is to make our American friends feel more at home. And then we secretly roll our eyes behind their backs when they wear a short, floral frock.

"Hmmm . . . ," our interior monologues say. "Guess she couldn't step it up and splurge for a BCBG evening gown."

It's true. We think our weddings are better than your weddings. If there's one thing our immigrant class would like to contribute to this country, it's fancier dresses and more dancing at your receptions. You're welcome, America.

Our traditional wedding ceremonies are nothing like the standard Western nuptials. For starters, the bride and groom are required to sit during the ceremony, usually facing away from the guests and toward what's called the sofreh aghd, or the traditional wedding altar. During the ceremony, many of the married female guests are invited to the altar to hold up a lace sheet over the couple and take turns grinding giant sugar cubes atop the sheet. This is supposed to symbolize a sweet life for the newlyweds. It's feminine and beautiful, but there's also some hurt feelings among the married women who aren't invited to partake in the tradition because, well, their unions suck and no one wants the bad juju. Traditionally, the groom says *baleh* (yes) right away when asked if he takes the bride to be his wife. But the bride keeps the guests in suspense by not answering the question until the third time it's been posed. Once she finally says *baleh*, the entire room erupts in cheers.

This particular portion of the wedding ceremony turns gender roles in the Iranian culture on their head. To me, the tradition suggests that it's the woman in the relationship who needs to make her mind up about the man. He's eager to commit, and she's too busy contemplating what she really wants out of life. It's a brief moment of female empowerment, which unfortunately isn't always ingrained in other arenas of our culture. To see more traditional gender roles play out, just go to a dinner party at a Persian person's house and watch as the women wash dishes after dinner and the men dick around and play backgammon.

On Sunday, Iran and US played against each other in the World Cup. Iran played awesome and won 2–1. It was so cool. My whole family was so happy. We all went to an Iranian café with flags and loud music. Later that day, we all went to Los Gatos and danced and sang. I've never felt so proud or so Iranian for that matter. There was so much comfort there. It made me wish I had more Iranian friends.

—Diary entry: July 1, 1998

Chapter Nine

◆ ★ ◆

Thick as Thieves

"Are you having a party, and if you are, why am I not invited?" Izzy asked me over the phone.

"I'm not having a party," I responded.

"Liar. It sounds like you have fifty people over."

"Oh, it's just two of my aunts," I replied. "They stopped by to see my mom."

"Why is it so loud? Are they fighting or something?"

"No. We're Persian. It's just the way we talk."

Whenever my friends called our house, they could barely make out my voice on the other end of the receiver and always assumed an impromptu gathering of a dozen or so relatives caused the background noise. What they eventually learned was that "quiet Iranian" is an oxymoron. I've never met one. We don't whisper or use inside voices. What's the point of saying anything if no one can hear you? Our opinions must be expressed at top volume in order for people to listen. You know when all the cohosts on a talk show speak at the same time and you don't understand what anyone is actually saying? The industry term for this is "cross talk." Well, that's what it was like to be around my mom's side of the family.

I couldn't tell you what it was like to be around my dad's side of the family. With the exception of Mamani, the Saedi contingent lived in Iran for the entirety of my teen years, so I only knew them through stories, letters and photographs we'd receive in the mail, and telephone conversations shouted at the top of our lungs to hear each other's voices through the shoddy long-distance connection. I never expressed it to my parents, but I dreaded the calls to Iran. I could always tell when my mom and dad were on an overseas call from the way they had to yell names into the receiver repeatedly until they heard someone else's voice on the other end of the line:

"FAFAR. FAFAR. FAFAR." My dad would bellow his younger sister's name over and over again.

"Ugh," I would vent to my sister. "They're calling Iran. Again."

It wasn't that I didn't want to talk to my relatives; it was that I didn't know what to say. When my parents handed me the phone, I would stretch the cord (yes, phones had cords) as far as it would go for privacy. My Farsi wasn't what it used to be, and I was ashamed of my now-thick American accent. I couldn't hide the fact that I was no longer like them. I wanted to have meaningful conversations with my grandma and aunts that captured my sassy humor and penchant for sarcasm, but I couldn't communicate much beyond the usual Farsi phrases:

"Delam yek zareh shodeh." (Literal translation: "My heart has turned into a tiny speck," which is just a fancy way to say "I really miss you.")

"Jotoon khaley kholly." (Literal translation: "Your place is very empty," which is just a fancy way to say "I really miss you.")

"Be omideh deedar." (Literal translation: "I hope to see you soon." We said this even though it had been years since we last saw each other, and we knew there were no visits on the horizon.)

On those phone calls, my limited vocabulary probably made me sound just like a teenage Siri. I'm sure my family in Iran wondered why I followed the same predictable script for every conversation. It wasn't until adulthood that several family members would become regular fixtures in my life, some of them finally moving to the States and others traveling here more frequently. My cousin Mehdi, who still lives in Tehran with his wife and kids, made his first trip to America in 2015. So when we said *"Be omideh deedar"* on those phone calls, we had to keep the hope alive for decades before we saw each other. While the Muslim ban was tied up in the courts, Mehdi was denied a visa to visit us, and also his parents, who now reside in California.

But while I was forced into isolation from my dad's family

back in the day, I still had more relatives living in the Bay Area than most of my American friends. My mom's entire side of the family (the Sanjideh contingent) moved to America after the revolution, and the majority of them followed my dayee Mehrdad to the Bay Area. Each family's escape plan from Iran would have amounted to disastrous consequences if it didn't go as planned. All of our departures from the country were dangerous, abrupt, and mostly illegal. There was no time to carefully sift through our prized possessions or to label neatly packed boxes. There were no raucous and lively farewell parties or cakes that read "America or Bust." We had no choice but to give the Middle East an Irish good-bye. But at least the Saedis got to take an airplane out of the country. One of my aunts had to hide in the back of a truck with her husband and two young children until they were driven miles to the Iran-Pakistan border. They made the rest of the trip on foot in the dead of night, hiking through mountains and rough terrain, terrified that they would be caught and thrown in jail. They were just like the von Trapp family, except they didn't wear clothes made from curtains or sing catchy songs about raindrops on roses and whiskers on kittens. They made it to Pakistan and eventually moved to Portugal, where they lived until they were able to come to America.

In Iran, the Sanjidehs were an upper-middle-class family. They were raised on a grand scale, living in a lavish home with maids and servants catering to their every whim. But they left their wealth behind when they moved to America, settling instead for tiny apartments and whatever jobs they could get. It was a riches-to-rags kind of story, but everyone found different paths to getting permanent residency in America. I had an aunt who went as far as divorcing her husband and briefly marrying an American family friend so that she could get a green card. But that option didn't sit well with my parents. Eventually, we became the only members of the Sanjideh clan who lived in the country illegally, as we patiently waited for updates on the adjustment-of-status applications we'd filed through my uncle and grandma.

In the beginning, family was the only thing we had in California. Most of us didn't speak the language (my mom says I learned English from watching television), and we had trouble adjusting to new customs. One day, I came home from kindergarten confused by the fact that none of my new friends wanted me to smother them with kisses. It's customary for Iranians to greet each other with a kiss on both cheeks, but American six-year-olds thought no one had taught me about "personal space." My mom gently told me that Americans preferred to greet each other with a simple "hello" or a friendly wave and handshake. To this day, any public displays of affection make me flinch. I also had more family than I was even aware of. When my kindergarten teachers informed me that my cousin had just joined our class, I blankly stared at the little boy they introduced me to.

"He's *not* my cousin," I said.

I'd never seen him before in my life. It turned out that he was my cousin's cousin, and my parents hadn't bothered to tell me he'd enrolled in my kindergarten class.

The eighties weren't the most ideal time to be a Persian in America. With the hostage crisis still fresh in the country's minds, we were public enemy number one. The news footage of Iranians protesting in the streets, burning the American flag, and screaming "DEATH TO AMERICA" didn't really do much to bolster our image. And then came the Iran-Contra scandal, which was the vanilla ice cream on the poop pie. But my parents tried to teach us to ignore any negative perceptions of our homeland. We knew the media didn't define our culture. What the news didn't show was that we were a passionate people who loved art and music and poetry. A people who came up with any excuse to throw a party and danced with their hips and shoulders in full swing. And who, above all, put family before anything.

"We're all we have," my parents would remind us. "Our family is the most important thing in life. Never forget that."

I mistakenly thought it was that way for everyone. I assumed my friends also came with a tribe of outspoken aunts, uncles, and cousins they saw on a regular basis. But when my friends would tell me they had cousins they'd never met—cousins who lived within an hour's drive—I couldn't help thinking: What is wrong with these cold and detached people? I didn't understand the concept of a "family reunion." Our family was always together. There was no reason to reunite. We were regular fixtures at each other's birthday parties, graduations, and weddings. We were the people who not only lived next door to one aunt but down the block from another. If we could have pooled our resources and bought a compound, we would have happily lived on the same plot of land. We'd been displaced by a war and a revolution, but at least we were displaced together.

I grew up among nineteen first cousins, and they each played a pivotal role in my childhood and teen years. Most of them had several years on me, and I could never shake the feeling that they were privy to family secrets and scandals that I was too young and innocent to know about. To me, they were more than cousins. They were an extended family of siblings, and I was the resident little sister. Some of them corrupted me with nicotine, drugs, and alcohol. Others taught me about sex and the importance of masturbation. One even made my wildest dreams come true by introducing me to the love of my life. (More on that later. Hint: he's a movie star.)

We were a motley crew of immigrant kids with vastly different personalities (think the cast of *The Breakfast Club*), but with one common thread keeping us permanently entwined. None of our friends knew what it was like to be raised by Iranian immigrants. None of our friends knew what it was like to *be* an immigrant. No one else understood the intricacies of our family and what our parents had to overcome just so we could live in America. The struggle was real, and it bonded us forever.

If there's one person in our family who deserves the credit for the close-knit relationships between us cousins, it's Dayee Mehrdad, otherwise known as the true patriarch of our massive brood. Mehrdad Sanjideh is a short man with

Dayee Mehrdad and his trusty Tupperware.

a charming and sophisticated personality. He keeps strange hours and prefers to eat his dinner late at night with a gin martini, so he brings his own Tupperware to parties.

There's nothing he loves more than being in the center of a dance circle. He dated models and actresses and romanced his stunning American wife after standing behind her in line to use the phone at Heathrow Airport. At the time, my aunt Geneva was trying to find a hotel in London, because the friends she'd planned to visit were suddenly unreachable. My notoriously impatient uncle told her that if she let him use the phone, he'd find her a hotel. He spent the weekend wooing her, and they were married just a few days later. He eventually moved his family from Tehran to Saratoga, California, in the seventies, and we moved in with them when we arrived in America. Shortly thereafter, he started a successful appraisal company with my dayee Shahrdad, and over the years, they employed nearly every member of our large family. Our relatives regularly went to him for advice on their businesses, rocky marriages, or dysfunctional relationships with their children. If our family had a mantra, it would be "What Would Mehrdad Do?"

Well, Mehrdad woke up one day and decided that he wanted his nieces and nephews to grow up as close to each other as he was with his cousins in Iran. And it became his life's purpose to make that happen. From the time I was seven years old, he planned elaborate gatherings for us at least once a year. We referred to ourselves as the BAD Club, and each letter in the acronym represented our relationship with him. The *B* stood for "baba," the *A* stood for "amoo," and the *D* stood for "dayee." Our cousins club started with day trips to places like Haight-Ashbury in San Francisco, the Egyptian museum in downtown San Jose, or (no joke) the racetrack at Golden Gate Fields. But eventually, one single afternoon together didn't feel like enough time and the tradition evolved into weekend sleepovers at my uncle's house. We'd spend the days swimming, barbecuing, and brainstorming sketch ideas we would later put on video for posterity. The videos always started the same way: with each of us entering the room one by one, waving at the camera and introducing ourselves. We were like our own Persian variety show. One sketch included a party sequence where we imitated our parents, but our masterpiece was the Persian *Jerry*

Springer Show. Naturally, my uncle would play the Persian Jerry Springer, and the rest of us took turns playing talk show guests and the rowdy audience members who shouted *"Es-springer!"* (the Persian-accent pronunciation of Springer) on repeat. The video ended with Persian Jerry *E*springer giving his final thought from a toilet seat. Once we grew older and drifted off to different cities, the notion of a "family reunion" no longer seemed ridiculous. So my uncle started a bank account to help fund our gatherings and pay for air travel for those of us who no longer lived near the Bay Area. Most recently, he treated all his nieces and nephews, and their spouses, to a three-day cruise to Mexico.

Aside from my uncle, there were four other people who bonded my cousins and me together. Benny Andersson, Björn Ulvaeus, Agnetha Fältskog, and Anni-Frid Lyngstad were the members of a little-known Swedish band from the 1970s called ABBA. Here's the thing. When you're raised by immigrants, they don't introduce you to American pop culture. As kids, we usually listened to Iranian musicians. My sister and I would always groan that we much preferred to dance around the house to Madonna or Michael Jackson, but my parents were too busy rocking out to Persian singers like Googoosh or Ebi. There was only one English-singing pop group that played on our family boom box, and that was ABBA. Not everyone fully understands the true power of ABBA, but you'll be hard-pressed to find an Iranian who doesn't love their entire catalog of music. To us, they were right up there with the Beatles. They had songs we could dance to at family parties, and ballads that could send you into a black hole of sadness. Their lyrics were about love, heartbreak, guys named Fernando, and places called Waterloo.

Even though ABBA was famous years before I was born, I listened to them religiously as a teen. I didn't exactly advertise this to any members of the opposite sex. Certainly not Evan Parker, who only listened to respectable classic rock bands. But I turned my American girlfriends onto ABBA, and they became totally obsessed. Izzy and I were the queens of falling in love with guys who didn't love us back, and nothing else quite captured our heartbreak the way songs like "The Winner Takes It All" or "One of Us" did. If our cousins club was one of our most tried-and-true traditions, then ABBA was a close second. "Dancing Queen" plays at every family wedding, and my female cousins and I push our way onto the dance floor to link arms and sway in a circle together. Sadly, ABBA doesn't tour anymore—they even turned down a billion-dollar offer for a concert. Both couples divorced in the eighties and the end of their marriages marked the breakup of the band. But their music lives on, thanks in great part to Iranians everywhere.

It's no coincidence that the biggest die-hard ABBA fans among us were also my greatest role models growing up. Neda and Mitra were best friends who were cut from a very different cloth, and I wanted to cherry-pick their greatest qualities so I could be the perfect combination of the two of them. My cousin Neda is eight years my senior, but she always spoke to me as if I were on her level. She had a way of making me feel like we were the same age, even though I was still in high school and she was a workingwoman in her twenties. She was also one of the kids hiding in the back of a truck headed for Pakistan. After living near each other our whole lives, I was gutted when Neda's parents moved their family to Colorado, but Neda lasted only a year in another state before she decided to return to the Bay Area. Samira had gone away to college, and we had an extra bedroom in our house, so my parents let her stay with us until she found her own place.

With Neda temporarily living with us, it felt like I had an older sister again. When she learned that I took the public bus home from school, she insisted on picking me up every

Hanging out with my cousin Neda before my high school formal. (This dress will be important later.)

day. She always arrived promptly in her blue Ford Escort, with a Cappuccino Blast from Baskin-Robbins waiting for me in the front seat. I sucked it down even though the high caffeine content gave me serious anxiety and terrible diarrhea. My group of friends loved Neda. She listened to stories about the boys we loved and the girls we hated, and offered sage and thoughtful advice. Neda was mature beyond her years and had a maternal side even as a child. She was polite and well mannered, and at family dinners was the first girl cousin up from her seat to clear the table and wash the dishes. The rest of our parents looked at us kids and wondered why we couldn't be more like Neda. Who could blame them? She was a perfect human.

If Neda was considered the "good girl" in the family, then my cousin Mitra was the rebellious black sheep. She and Neda were only a few years apart in age, and even though their personalities were wildly dissimilar, they were inseparable. Mitra was my dayee Mehrdad's daughter, and half-Iranian. With her fair skin, bright green eyes, and auburn hair, you'd never know she wasn't just another white girl. All through high school, I referred to her as my "cool cousin." She always had a string of hot skater boyfriends, an adorable nose piercing, and a shoe rack full of Doc Marten boots. Just like Winona Ryder, she could totally pull off a pixie cut. So what if she had a tendency to run away from home and go missing for days with her boyfriend? The girl marched to the beat of her own drum. She didn't care what the elders in the family thought of her. I felt cooler just by association. I smoked cigarettes with Mitra. I ditched family parties with her so we could drive to a nearby park and listen to her boyfriend play guitar. She promised me that when I graduated from high school, I could skip college altogether and move in with her. I knew my parents would never go for it, but it was nice to know I had options if my undocumented status meant a bachelor's degree wasn't in my future.

But Neda had her rebellious moments, too. She was just better at hiding them. When I was thirteen, they both decided it would be really fun to get me drunk. I suppose corrupting me was everyone's favorite pastime in my family. My parents were out of town, so Neda and Mitra came over to our house with a bottle of vodka and a two-liter of 7Up. My sister was a veteran drinker by then, but I'd never had more than a few sips of wine and beer. I'd certainly never had hard liquor before. It was Saint Neda who introduced us to her favorite drink: vodka poppers. The recipe was simple: two parts vodka, one part 7Up. You'd stick your hand over the shot and bang it on the counter, and once it started fizzing, you tossed it back. I could barely taste any of the booze on the way down. I was tipsy and happy and seriously shocked when virginal Neda confessed to me that she'd been sexually active for a while (Samira, our cousin Leyla, and Mitra were already in the know). It hurt to know that for the past year, she'd made comments about being inexperienced for no one's benefit but my own. But I was glad that with high school just around the corner, I was deemed mature enough to know my cousin's biggest secrets.

In the photo below, taken that night, you can't see the image of the guy on my T-shirt, but it's a picture of a young Ethan Hawke. My sister knew I had an enormous crush on him and had my favorite magazine photo of him put on a T-shirt as a birthday present. You may know him as the guy who played the dad in *Boyhood,* but he used to be a Gen X icon. As far as I was concerned, no other actor could play vulnerable quite like Ethan Hawke, and I fell madly in love with him. I read every interview and saw all his movies. When *Reality Bites* came out, I was almost angry that other girls were now jumping on the Ethan Hawke bandwagon. My devotion to him started during his *Dead Poets Society* days. I loved him so much that I named my beloved goldfish after him.

My sister on the left, me in the middle, Neda on the right.

Poor Ethan (the fish) wasn't very well taken care of. We'd bought him for our Persian New Year altar known as the *haft-seen*.* Goldfish represented the end of the astral year. Once the holiday passed and the altar was put away, Ethan lived in a small glass mixing bowl that we kept by the sink on our kitchen counter. Izzy was always bewildered by Ethan's survival. Her mom had bought her two fish, with a gorgeous aquarium to house them in, and they'd both died within months. Despite serious neglect on my part, Ethan had been alive for two years.

"It's because he represents my enduring love for Ethan Hawke," I would explain to my friends without a hint of irony (which I can define, because I've seen *Reality Bites*).

As much as I loved every one of my cousins and had significant relationships with each of them, I have Mitra to thank for one of the best days of my life. It was my junior year of high school, and Mitra persuaded my parents to let me play hooky for the day. She refused to tell me where we were going, but after driving for a half hour on 280 North, I suspected we were headed into San Francisco. With no knowledge of our plans for the day, I still decided to wear an outfit worthy of Mitra's coolness. An old pair of Levi's that Izzy had given me from the 1970s, a black tank top, black Doc Marten lace-up boots, and the pièce de résistance: a maroon velvet blazer that I'd found

---

Haft-seen literally translates to "seven *s*'s." The altar includes seven items that begin with the letter *s*, all with their own symbolic meaning. It also includes a bevy of other non-*s*-related objects. For instance, "fish" is *mahi* in Farsi.

on the rack of a thrift store. Trust me, velvet blazers were all the rage.

We had a few hours to kill when we arrived in San Francisco, so Mitra took me out to lunch and we roamed the crowded city streets. We stopped at her boyfriend's tiny apartment, where I bravely pretended to inhale a little pot, and then we continued on our way. We strolled down Market Street and approached the massive Virgin Records (a place that used to sell cassette tapes, CDs, and books) on the corner. Mitra pretended like there was a CD she wanted to pick up, but when I followed her inside, she pointed me toward a sign and said: "What if I told you *this* is what we were doing today?"

I nearly fainted. I couldn't speak. I wanted to burst into tears. The sign had a photo of Ethan Hawke, along with the cover of his debut novel, *The Hottest State*. He was going to be there in a mere hour to read a chapter from his book and sign copies. I was about to meet the love of my life. I was nearly shaking as we walked up to the register, and Mitra bought us each a copy of Hawke's book. The cover was a beautiful watercolor of a dripping green heart, with one symbolic drop of red paint. Some critics rolled their eyes at Hawke's efforts to become a writer, but I just thought it made him even sexier. He was more than just a guy who recited other people's lines of dialogue. He was thoughtful and intelligent and quite possibly the voice of an entire generation.

"I can't believe this," I whispered to Mitra as we waited for the reading to start.

We were among the first to arrive, so we snagged seats in the second row. The chairs began to fill up, and finally, after what felt like several tortured hours, Ethan Hawke walked down the aisle and took a seat in the front at a microphone. I can still remember what he was wearing: a forest-green suit with a black T-shirt underneath. Back when there was no Twitter or Instagram, you had no clue what your favorite celebrities were doing at any given moment, but I remember watching him and thinking, "I know exactly where Ethan Hawke is right now."

The moment became even more surreal as I scanned the rest of the audience and noticed a beaming Uma Thurman on the sidelines. I'd never been so jealous of any human being before in my life. I knew everything about celebrities (in fact, Izzy's mom referred to me as the "information superhighway"), but news of the Hawke-Thurman pairing hadn't reached the magazines yet. Gossip columns had not found their way to the Internet, so we relied solely on monthly magazines for the latest on whom our favorite celebrities were dating.

I tried to stay in the moment and focus on Ethan's raspy voice as he read a chapter from his book, but I was way too nervous. Once the reading wrapped, we were told to form an orderly line to get our books signed. Mitra stood in front of me. I tried to think of the perfect, most memorable thing to say to Ethan, but my brain had turned to mush. I stood in awe as Mitra casually greeted him and told him how cool it was to hear a writer interpret his own words aloud. I watched as Ethan's face lit up, and he agreed. There was nothing sixteen-year-old me could say to him that would sound as smart and perceptive. I finally approached the table, and Mitra hung around nearby to observe the moment. All I could think was that my parents were right. In America, *anything* was possible. In America, dreams really did come true. I opened my mouth and carefully uttered, "I hope I can write like you one day."

He looked up from the book and said, "Thank you. Thanks so much for coming."

If you think my memories of the day might be inaccurate more than twenty years later, here's the moment described in my diary:

October 29, 1996
Finally, he walked in. He looked so beautiful, but skinnier than I thought he was. His hair was short and messy, and he had facial hair. He looked really nervous, and it was so cute because he couldn't get the microphone to work at first . . . then he read aloud chapter 19 of his book, which was so cool . . . Then we got in line to get our books signed . . . I was so nervous when I went up to him. I told him I thought it was really good, and that I hope I can write like him one day . . . I want him so bad.

The next day, I checked on my goldfish, Ethan, but to my dismay, he was floating on his side in his small mixing bowl. Ethan was dead. He'd served his purpose. I had met my number one celebrity crush, and now my fish could peacefully swim across the rainbow bridge.

I was sad to see Ethan the fish go, but meeting his namesake had been the perfect send-off. From then on, spending my days at school would feel like a total waste of time. There was a great big world out there, and I wanted to explore it. I knew I was lucky to have older cousins to take

Cousins and spouses piled into an elevator on a cruise ship, 2015.

me on adventures that included meeting my literary heroes and drinking tasty vodka concoctions. As far as I was concerned, my dayee Mehrdad had already succeeded at his life's purpose. My cousins and I were thick as thieves, and we would stay that way even when we grew up and started our own families.

I just feel like I'm not good at anything. I know I'm probably just being too hard on myself, but I'm a little annoyed at myself, my personality, everything—except for my family. That's one thing I'm always thankful to have.

—Diary entry: May 13, 1995

Chapter Ten

◆ ★ ◆

Divorce: Illegal Immigrant–Style

Here's a scenario I frequently witnessed during my adolescence: My dad, at the wheel of the car, with my mom sitting in the passenger seat. Me, in the back seat, usually in the center so I could lean forward with my seat belt on to control the radio and turn up the volume anytime a good song came on. Apropos of nothing, my mom's and dad's hands would meet somewhere near the air conditioner unit, and they'd hold on to each other until my dad had to make a tricky turn or merge onto the freeway and needed to keep both hands positioned on the wheel. Inevitably, over the course of wherever we were driving to, their hands would find their way back to each other again. It never occurred to me that those brief displays of affection between one's parents were rare or special or that they even required hard work to achieve. I took these moments for granted, but from where I was sitting, I got to observe a stable, functional, and joyful relationship. And that's precisely why it was so shocking when I learned my mom and dad had gotten a divorce. I may have buried the lead, but I need to give you twenty years of epically romantic context before we revisit the end of their marriage.

From the day my parents were reunited in America after the Iranian Revolution, they never spent much time apart from each other. They co-ran their luggage business, which meant they spent their days at work together and then spent their evenings at home commiserating over dissatisfied customers or certain suitcases that were damaged beyond repair. My dad generally got home a few hours later than my mom, but as a rule she never ate dinner without him. Even though we had a dining table, my sister, brother, and I would plop place mats on the floor and eat our dinners while watching sitcoms. By the time my dad got home and my parents ate, it was sometimes close to ten at night. We rarely ate dinner around the table as a family. In fact, I remember being confused anytime I went to dinner at my childhood best friend Megan's house and realized they (a) ate dinner at 6:00 p.m., which was considered early for foreigners like us; (b) had rituals like asking to be excused from the table; and (c) drank milk with dinner instead of water or soda. A creamy beverage with savory food? Had Americans lost their damn minds? Milk is meant for cereal and desserts. As a bonus, I also learned there was a difference between napkins and tissues. In our home, we used Kleenex to wipe our mouths. Megan and I met in second grade, but her family would eventually move to Massachusetts and I would visit her during the summers. Her parents were among the first to know that my family was undocumented. When Megan's dad told my mom that they wanted to take us to Canada for a few days during one of my visits, my mom had to politely decline and explain that I wasn't allowed to leave the country.

Compared to those of Megan's family, our family rituals were either less rigid or nonexistent. I loved that my siblings and I got to watch the TGIF lineup while we ate dinner. I also respected the fact that my mom never let my dad eat alone. Apparently, this was one ritual she'd started in the early days of their marriage. I didn't quite understand how they still had so much to discuss over a meal of zereshk polo,* considering they'd spent the entire day together, but theirs was not the kind of relationship that was filled with comfortable silences. They never seemed to run out of things to say to each other, which made it all the more astounding that they'd known each other for a total of two weeks before they got married.

I used to flaunt this fact to my friends at school. I thought it was *so* romantic. "It was love at first sight," I would tell everyone. "When you know, you just know." But there was one minor detail I left out every time I told the story of how my parents met. I conveniently forgot (or refused) to mention that they had an . . . arranged marriage. I was embarrassed by this detail. Maybe I had bought into the Western depictions

_____

*One of my favorite Persian dishes, consisting of rice with saffron, chicken, and barberries.

of what it meant to fall in love. All my favorite movies started with "boy meets girl." They did not start with "boy's parents and girl's parents think they'd be a good match and *then* boy marries girl." And while my parents never liked to dwell on this particular aspect of their courtship, they didn't just stumble across each other in a freak thunderstorm or at a costume party or at a friend's disastrous wedding. Instead, their families introduced them to each other.

The year was 1974. My dad was a twenty-eight-year-old mechanical engineering student at Louisiana State University. He was probably one of the oldest undergraduates at college, but he joined the military after high school in Iran and didn't move to Baton Rouge until his early twenties. He also put himself through school, which meant working odd jobs as a waiter and a bus driver to pay his rent and his tuition. Balancing school with work made it impossible for him to finish his studies in four years. He still loves to tell stories from his youth living in America, particularly the moments that English words and phrases got lost in translation. There was the time his boss at the restaurant asked him to "give him a hand," and my dad, thinking he was being praised for a hard day's work, responded by excitedly shaking his boss's hand. During the summer of '74, he returned to Iran to visit with family and take a break from his grueling schedule.

Back in Tehran, my mom was only nineteen and had spent the last year begging her overbearing father to send her to university in London. Her older brother (my dayee Shahrdad) was already a college student in London, and he'd agreed to let her move in with him. At first, my grandfather was totally against the idea. He worried my mom and her brother would form an unholy alliance and do whatever the hell they wanted with the understanding that neither would report their dalliances to their parents. After a lot of persuading, he finally relented and my mom started making arrangements to move to Europe. But her plans went out the window when my dad walked into her life.

Though they hadn't met in person, my mom had heard a great deal about Ali Saedi from Baton Rouge. There was only one degree of separation between them. My mom's older sister and my dad's younger sister had become close friends after marrying into the same family. They regularly shared photographs of my dad with my mom, subtly pointing out that he was single and that they'd make a great couple. Without the help of the Internet or dating apps, most people back then met their future spouses through family or mutual friends, but months of courtship usually followed before getting engaged. In my parents' case, they dated for a week, then spent the following week planning their wedding.

Apparently, one reason my grandfather supported the union was that it meant my mom would ditch her plans to move to London. The idea of her getting married and moving to America was a lot easier to digest than that of her moving to Europe as a single girl. Even though some aspects of the country were more liberal in the 1970s, arranged marriages were actually more commonplace than they are in contemporary Iran. Today, in Iran's urban areas, the great majority of the younger generation tend to meet their significant others on their own. But in smaller cities and villages, arranged marriages are still the norm, particularly introductions initiated by parents.

Most of my aunts also had arranged marriages, but in my mom and dad's case it was more of a strong suggestion from each set of parents than a dramatic mandatory proposition like when the Capulets tried to force Juliet into marrying Paris.

"Yes," my mom explained to me over the years, "technically, we had an arranged marriage, but I was never forced to marry your dad. I had a choice."

This is true. Neither of them was looking for a spouse at the time. If my mom decided that Ali didn't live up to his photographs or that he was an ogre with halitosis and no discernible sense of humor, she could have politely refused to marry him. Both my parents had a say in the decision, but they swear they were instantly taken with each other. The chemistry was undeniable, and neither of them was prepared to walk away from it. Somehow my dad's seventies sideburns and bushy 'stache didn't deter my mom from wanting to reproduce with him. I asked her recently what she liked about him, and she said that aside from the physical attraction, my dad had a warm personality and an infectious sense of humor. My dad was won over by my mom's zest for adventure and her independent spirit. After a few days of "dating," she told him that she didn't want to give up her plans to move to London just for a guy who wanted to get married because his parents thought it was a good idea. She was in no rush to shack up, and only wanted my dad to go through with the marriage if he genuinely thought she was someone he could fall in love with.

And so, fourteen days after my parents first laid eyes on each other, friends and family gathered to celebrate their union. It's hard for me to imagine why my mom wasn't in a state of constant anxiety during this period in her life. She was still a teenager who'd never lived apart from her parents. Aside from one kiss with a neighbor, she'd never dated

August 22, 1974.

anyone. But her wedding night would end with losing her virginity to a man she'd known for only a couple of weeks. I think it's fair to say that's batshit crazy.

My mom admits that nerves were part of the equation but says her doubts and anxieties were allayed by the excitement of starting a life with my dad. There was one slight glitch to happily ever after. Ten days after their wedding, he had to return to school, while my mom waited to get her visa so she could join him in Louisiana. They spent an agonizing two months apart, writing each other letters to stay in touch. Each of those letters is preserved in an album, and one of my biggest regrets is that I'm close to illiterate in Farsi and have never been able to pore through their words to each other.

During their forced time away from each other, my grandfather (Ata Baba, as his children and grandchildren called him) was tasked with getting my mom's paperwork in order, but he had a demanding job and a slew of other obligations that slowed down her visa. He passed away before I was born, but I've always wondered if he was purposely stalling so he could keep his youngest daughter in the same country with him for as long as possible. One day, after my mom grumbled that he needed to make her visa a priority, he looked at her and said, "You've been my daughter for *nineteen* years. You've been his wife for *one* month. Why are you in such a hurry to leave us?"

My grandfather had an imposing presence, but he was a devoted father and was well respected by his peers. Among his children, he was known for being hotheaded and unpredictable, but equal parts loving. Had my mom known what the future held, I think she would have soaked up those last days with her own family and wouldn't have been in such a rush to leave home. Four years later, her dad would unexpectedly die of a heart attack at the age of fifty-six, leaving behind his wife, five children, and eight grandchildren.

Eventually, my mom received a visa, and she and my dad finally got their own version of a romantic comedy of errors. My mom's journey across the globe started when she flew from Tehran to London to spend a couple of days with her brother. She would next get on a flight to Atlanta and meet my dad at the airport so they could fly to Baton Rouge together. Since my mom couldn't speak much English, she didn't want to make any airport connections by herself, so my dad planned to fly to Atlanta to pick her up. But when my uncle took her to Heathrow to catch her flight to Atlanta, the airport employees informed her that the original flight time had been moved up a couple hours and that she'd missed the plane. This meant she was about to experience her worst nightmare:

Heathrow ⟶ JFK ⟶ Atlanta.

My mom had heard JFK was massive, and she was terrified to navigate the airport's terminals on her own. Not only did she barely speak the language, but she'd also never spent much time outside of Iran. My dayee Shahrdad got my mom on the plane in Heathrow, begged the flight attendants to look after her, and sent her on her way. Without cell phones or email, there was no way for Shahrdad to reach my dad to tell him about the flight change. Meanwhile, my dad landed at the Atlanta airport eager to reconnect with his wife, only to be told that the flight from Heathrow had gotten in two hours earlier and there was no Shohreh Saedi on the plane. He had no idea what was going on. Was it cold feet? Had she been kidnapped? Was she trapped in the wrong terminal, worried that her new husband had abandoned her? For the next few hours, he frantically searched the airport, trying to find my mom. When her flight from JFK finally landed in Atlanta, my mom did the same thing . . . wondering how on earth she'd ever find my dad. Eventually, she spotted him walking toward her, tears of panic streaming down his face. And thus began their love story. They would live in Louisiana for the next two years; when my dad graduated from college, they returned to Iran, where they remained until their escape in 1982. My dad spent most of that last year at LSU skipping classes so he could be with my mom, who wondered why getting a degree didn't actually require attending lectures.

Growing up, I was proud of and intimidated by my parents' relationship. I loved that they were the type of couple who could make each other laugh with one look or inside joke, and that they craved each other's company enough to go on date nights that included dinner and dancing. To the rest of our extended family, they became the symbol of a happy marriage. Like every couple, they had their ups and downs, but we kids were rarely made aware of the struggles (mostly caused by strained finances and our rocky immigration status). When sixteen-year-old me, who'd suffered from

My dad's graduation from LSU in 1976.

chronic bouts of unrequited love, looked at them, all I could wonder was, Will I *ever* be this happy? And that's precisely why I was left emotionally discombobulated when I found out that my parents had secretly gotten divorced.

"Is love just a sham?" was my first reaction, and then my parents quickly explained that they'd been advised by a legal consultant to get a divorce so that my mom, sister, and I could apply to get a green card through my grandmother. We had already filed for permanent residency through my uncle, but once my grandmother became a green card holder, we decided to see if another application would be a speedier option. But there was one catch. As it turned out, you can apply to get a green card through a parent (who's a permanent resident and *not* an American citizen) only if you're single. Thus, if my mom wanted to apply for residency through her mom, then my dad had to technically be out of the picture.

"No problem," my parents thought. "We'll just get a divorce. Marriage is just a piece of paper!"

The divorce took place in 1992, just a couple years shy of their twentieth wedding anniversary. Their commitment meant a great deal to them, but they were desperate for us to become legal residents, and if getting divorced meant alleviating our #IllegalImmigrantProblems, then so be it. But ending a marriage in California would take at least a year, and we didn't have that kind of time. So my baba and maman made the four-hour drive to Reno, Nevada, to secure a quickie divorce.

Once they arrived in Reno, their first plan of attack was to . . . stop at a restaurant to get a bite to eat. Maybe it was kismet, but they spotted an elderly Iranian man dining with his son and decided to rope them into their kooky divorce plan. That's one of the bonuses of moving to a foreign country. Fellow immigrants from your homeland are more than willing to pay it forward and pitch in to make sure the INS doesn't detain you. They explained their predicament to the man and his son, who agreed to serve as witnesses to their divorce.

Iranians kind of have no shame. We're instantly bonded by our histories and our willingness to ask strangers for ridiculous favors. Luckily, the old man, Nasser, had no moral qualms about their divorce of convenience and agreed to help. Nasser and his son followed my parents to the county clerk's office, but once they got there, my dad realized he'd left his wallet at the restaurant. By then, poor Nasser thought he'd been roped into an intricate con. Eventually, my dad returned with his wallet, and the divorce went off without any more hitches. Thanks in great part to the lax divorce laws in Nevada, my parents were officially single again.

I would like to let the record show that Ali and Shohreh probably had the *most* amicable divorce in the history of divorces. Gwyneth Paltrow and Chris Martin had nothing on them. They didn't tell us kids about the divorce till after it happened, and when they finally mentioned it, they claimed it was a small price to pay if it ended our immigration struggles. It would hopefully mean we'd get green cards in the next couple of years, my parents would remarry each other, and my dad would become a permanent resident as well. I didn't take much comfort in their explanation. My immigrant child guilt complex was boiling over. It infuriated me that two people who loved each other as much as they did had to split up in the eyes of the law, just so they could remain in the United States. Even though they were willing to try anything, I'd personally reached peak frustration levels at our country's complex and seemingly arbitrary immigration laws. I wanted to get on the first flight to Washington, DC, and storm the Capitol. But I didn't, because any form of criminal activity would get me deported. I knew our options were slim, but it felt like my mom and dad's love story was tainted. How could I continue to brag about their two-week courtship when I secretly knew they were no longer married?

As it turned out, the divorce was all for naught. For reasons beyond our control, we never ended up getting a green card through my grandmother. And in 1997, when it looked like our adjustment of status (through the application sponsored by my uncle) was nearing consideration, our new lawyer nearly lost his mind when he learned my parents had gotten divorced several years earlier.

"You have to get remarried right away!" he told them. "If you don't, it will take even longer for Ali to get his green card."

They promptly took his advice, drove to city hall in San Jose, and "renewed their vows," with my uncle as their witness. So they knew each other for fourteen days before their first marriage, and twenty-three years before their second marriage. Even after they remarried, we knew there was still an uphill battle ahead to becoming American citizens. But for now, that didn't matter. We were all relieved the divorced years were behind us.

Today, when I grip my US passport and walk through airport security to travel overseas, knowing I'll be allowed to return, I always remind myself that this privilege came at a high cost. When I walk into a voting booth, I tell myself that this right came amid many sacrifices. My parents thought of the divorce as trading one piece of paper for another, and I try to compartmentalize it in the same way. But then I consider that nineteen-year-old girl waiting desperately for her visa to come through in Tehran so that she could start a life with her husband in America, and I feel myself getting angry again on her behalf. It'll never sit well that years later she had to end her happy, hard-earned marriage just to give her children a better life.

FREQUENTLY ASKED QUESTION #5
Why do Iranians always argue over the bill?

Persians have a famous ritual called *taarof*. It's so specific to our culture that there's no translation for it in English. The act of *taarof* is hard to explain, but here's an example. Two Iranians go out to dinner. The check comes. They both insist on paying the bill. They fight about it. They may try to pull the billfold out of each other's hands. They definitely cause a scene. It seems as though they're both desperate to treat the other to dinner, but mostly this is just their way of being polite. You must *taarof*. Another example: You're a guest in someone's house. They ask you if you'd like anything to eat. You politely decline. They keep asking. You keep politely declining. And then you finally relent, because you were actually hungry the whole time, but it seemed more polite not to make them go to the kitchen and bring you food.

If you ever want to see an Iranian's eyes bug out of their head, all you have to do is instantly accept their offer of treating you to dinner without argument. It's not that we don't expect to pay for dinner. It's that we expect you to put up a fight.

When I'm in school, I feel like the world is passing me by. I wonder what Brad Pitt is doing at this very second. I want to be famous. I just know I'm gonna be old, and I'm going to be thinking that all the things I've ever wanted to do or accomplish, I haven't done. My life is over. And I really miss my grandma.

—Diary entry: February 23, 1995

Chapter Eleven

⸻ ◆ ★ ◆ ⸻

I Am a Product of Incest

It's true. I really am. I suppose I'd prefer to be a product of incest than the alternative (not existing), but it's admittedly kind of weird. The incest is on my mom's side of the family, thanks to my grandmother, Mansoureh "Maman Soury"* Naficy. She had quite the tumultuous love life. My younger years and boy problems pale in comparison to what she dealt with. Her love affairs were far more steamy and complicated. If she had kept a journal, here's what a typical entry would have looked like:

Sometime in the 1940s
Something totally crazy and unexpected happened. I

---

*Soury is pronounced *SUE-ree*. If you want to nail the Persian accent, then roll the *r*.

fell in love with my husband's nephew! And he's in love with me, too. What do I do now?!

While most of my youth was spent pining away for Evan Parker, Maman Soury spent her younger days at the center of what may have been Iran's most scandalous love triangle, but there was a decent amount of turmoil in her life before Hurricane Extramarital Affair turned her world upside down. My grandmother became an orphan at the tender age of seven. Her mom died when she was four, and her dad passed away three years later. The responsibility of raising her fell to her older brothers, and her father's *other* wives. That's right. My great-grandfather was a full-fledged polygamist. The man was totally shady. He was an accomplished doctor who would treat patients in exchange for marrying their young and pretty daughters, some as young as thirteen or fourteen years old. This was a (sick) cultural norm.

Despite the void left by the death of her parents, my grandmother grew up to be an ambitious young woman. She was widely known for her intelligence, and she received her high school diploma at a time when education was not a priority for the female population in Iran. By the time she turned twenty-three, she gave in to societal norms and decided to get married to a first cousin she had never met. The marriage was arranged, but my grandmother didn't put up a fight. She knew she'd put off marriage for long enough, and she'd been told her future husband was a really nice guy. "What the heck," she thought. "Let's do this thing."

The *sofreh aghd* (reminder: the Iranian wedding altar) includes a variety of symbolic items, like eggs to represent fertility, fruit to represent a joyous life, and a mirror to represent a bright future for the married couple. Traditionally, the bride and groom glimpse their reflections throughout the ceremony. For my grandmother, the very first time she saw the face of the man she was marrying was in their wedding mirror. Her heart sank the moment her gaze fell on his reflection. She knew right then that she would never be attracted to him. (For the record, I've seen photographs and I thought he was a handsome guy.) Despite the lack of physical chemistry, her cousin-turned-husband lived up to his reputation as a compassionate and caring spouse who meant my grandmother no ill will. Together, they had three children. Fun fact: her husband already had a daughter from a previous marriage who would go on to marry my grandmother's brother. My family was as incestuous as the contestants on *Bachelor in Paradise*.

Overall, my grandmother felt content and safe in her marriage, but it lacked the kind of passionate love she always imagined for herself. And then, one summer, her husband's nephew moved in with them. By then, she was twenty-eight and the nephew was only twenty-one. He was the romantic type and instantly became enamored with his uncle's wife. He showered my grandmother with compliments, and for the first time in her life, she felt desirable. Eventually, they fell in love, and though she claimed they never acted on their feelings, they decided that they couldn't live without each other. There was only one solution: she would divorce her husband and marry his nephew.

In our day and age, you might give a cop-out excuse like "The heart wants what it wants," but keep in mind this was *Iran* in the *1940s*. Women did not leave their husbands, and they certainly did not run off with their husbands' nephews. It was a bold move on my grandmother's part, and though we could all revel in the romance of it, it was a love affair that destroyed multiple lives and scandalized an entire family. Everyone discouraged my grandmother from breaking off her marriage. And they especially discouraged the much younger nephew from marrying her. Relatives warned him that she was too old for him and that he was much better off finding an age-appropriate wife without the baggage of three children. But their advice fell on deaf ears. He refused to listen. He simply responded that he needed to breathe the same air that she breathed.

My grandmother wasn't quite as certain. In the middle of it all, with family members in a state of ire over their love affair, she got cold feet. But it was too late to undo the damage. Her husband couldn't forgive the indiscretion and didn't want to be with her anymore. Can you blame the guy? And so my grandmother followed her heart, dissolved her marriage, and got hitched to her ex-husband's nephew (who was technically her second cousin). The nephew was *my* grandfather Ata Baba.

I don't know if their torrid beginnings cast a dark shadow on them, but my grandparents' marriage was laced with hardship and tragedy. After her divorce, my grandmother's family essentially disowned her. Her youngest daughter (my khaleh Mina) went to live with her and her new husband, but she lost custody of her two oldest children (my khaleh Mandana and my dayee Mohammad), who would initially stay with their father. At the age of eleven, Khaleh Mandana began to display signs of an eating disorder, and doctors advised that she was better off living with her mother. Recently, my aunt revealed to me that once she was able to live

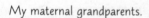

My maternal grandparents.

with her mother, she was terrified to eat, because she worried that as soon as she conquered her eating disorder and gained weight, she'd be forced to move back in with her dad. Of her three children from her first marriage, Mohammad was the only one who never lived with my grandmother after the divorce. Their separation was a void he struggled with through his adolescence and into adulthood. He and my grandmother still had a close bond, but he never had the benefit of being raised by his biological mother. The distance from her firstborn was one of my grandmother's many scarlet letters. Though she was allowed to visit him often, she was consumed by the guilt of living apart from him.

But it was another tragedy in her life that deepened the abyss of shame and grief she'd readily succumbed to. It took place on what began as a mundane afternoon in her home in Tehran. Like all life-changing events, it happened unexpectedly and without any foreshadowing. Everyone in the house was taking their midday nap when Mina, who was only six years old, woke up and quietly went into the backyard to rinse off some of her toy dishes in a small swimming pool. While my grandmother was still asleep, Mina fell in the pool and drowned. My grandmother discovered her body and tried to revive her, but it was too late.

Her romance with my grandfather came at the highest of costs. I can only imagine the daily what-ifs that monopolized her thoughts. What if she'd never left her husband in the first place? What if Mina hadn't come to live with her and my grandfather? Would she have grown up to have a long and happy life? If my grandma could have gone back to that summer when her husband's nephew moved into her house, would she have avoided falling in love with him? No one knows. I have vivid memories of her, as an old woman, regularly looking at a black-and-white photo of Mina and bursting into tears.

She would go on to have five more children with my grandfather. My mom was the youngest of the lot, but when my grandmother was pregnant with her, she debated whether she should terminate the pregnancy. Abortion was, and still is, illegal in Iran, but women were either able to find medical practitioners willing to perform one or would take the back-alley route. By then, my grandparents had a volatile relationship, plagued by the fact that my grandfather had engaged in an extramarital affair with a younger woman. As it turned out, their relatives had correctly predicted their fate: their age gap would lead to long-term problems in their marriage. The same intensity and passion that brought them together now fueled bitter fights, mostly surrounding Ata Baba's infidelity, which was why my grandmother worried that the stress of another child would permanently break their already fragile union. It was Mandana who begged and pleaded with her to carry my mom to term. My aunt was sixteen then and promised she would help raise the baby. Khaleh Mandana and I have always shared a special bond, and I'm certain our connection has to do with the fact that she essentially saved my life.

My grandparents would remain married for thirty-five years, until the day Ata Baba died of a heart attack. My mom says that despite their marital woes and my grandfather's wandering eye, they remained in love till the very end. Now, looking back, my mom thinks my grandmother went through bouts of clinical depression. She never got over the visceral grief of losing her daughter or the fact that she didn't raise her oldest child. There were also signs that my grandfather may have suffered from a mood disorder. During his upswings, everyone wanted to be in his presence, but during his downswings, he was known to cast a cold shadow.

While both my grandmothers led extraordinary lives marred by drama and tragedy, they were ultimately very different women. Maman Farideh liked her alone time and independence. On the flip side, Maman Soury never lived on her own after she moved to America. For the majority of the years she resided in the States, she lived with Khaleh Mehrzad and her family, but when they left California for Colorado, Maman Soury moved in with us. She lived in the Bay Area for over a decade, but she never learned to speak English beyond words like "please" and "thank you." She didn't have much motivation to learn the language. She never went anywhere alone and was surrounded by Farsi speakers at all times. But the language barrier didn't prevent her love of American television. *Wheel of Fortune* and *Days of Our Lives* (which also aired in Iran) were her two favorite programs. When it came to the latter, it was our job to translate the intricate plot twists and romantic entanglements. Whenever my Farsi failed me, I just made up what the characters were saying to each other with words I could remember. One of the high points of her life was the day she attended a taping of *Wheel of Fortune* and visited Vanna White's dressing room. My aunt Geneva's sister was Vanna White's neighbor and arranged the meet and greet.

Maman Soury was also a huge fan of Jell-O and sugar-free vanilla ice cream, which I was required to scoop up for her on a daily basis. Unlike Mamani, she was mostly sedentary and spent the bulk of her time on the couch. She had to appreciate the smaller things in life like food and TV. Her health was also a constant battle. She'd been a chain-smoker, and as she approached her eighties, she would spend weeks at a time in the hospital due to emphysema. The sterile hallways of the ICU and the scent of illness caused me bouts of anxiety when we'd visit her, but no matter how bad she looked, she always seemed to make a full recovery. I started to expect that every hospital stint would end with her returning home.

During the Christmas holidays in 1994, she'd been hospitalized again. This time, she seemed more out of it and delirious than during my other visits. It was the morphine,

Further proof that anything can happen in America.

195

my mom told me. She was in a lot of pain and the drugs were making her foggy. I figured that in a few days she'd be feeling better and we'd get to bring her home, but my siblings and I woke up on Christmas morning to discover that my parents were nowhere to be found. It could only mean they'd been called by the hospital to go see her in the middle of the night. We stared at our unopened Christmas gifts, wondering if we should selfishly tear through the wrapping paper or wait for my parents to come home so we could open our presents together.

Aside from my dayee Mehrdad, who had an American wife, we were the only other family among my relatives who bothered to celebrate Christmas. My parents worried we'd get teased by our classmates for not celebrating the holiday, so they decided to embrace the secular elements of Christmas (i.e., tree and presents) and to ignore the whole "birth of Christ" portion. There was one year that I remember opening our gifts only to make the startling discovery that we were *poor*. When all my friends were getting Pound Puppies and She-Ra figurines, my mom had wrapped up place mats and umbrellas that I recognized from our local drugstore. This particular year, I was hoping for a pricey pair of maroon Mary Jane Doc Martens, but fancy new shoes were suddenly the least of my concerns.

I distinctly remember the way the rest of that Christmas morning played out. I was wearing my oversize terry cloth Victoria's Secret bathrobe over pajamas while we waited for my parents to return home. In our family room, we had a large window with a view of the street and the entrance of our house. I spotted a few cars pull up and watched the procession of aunts and uncles walk toward our front door. Dayee Mohammad's wife was the first to greet me, and I asked her how my grandmother was doing.

"She's fine," she answered somberly. The relief I felt was instant.

But when my mom walked through the door shortly after, she pulled me into a hug and simply whispered, "She's gone." I immediately burst into tears and held on to my mom as we both cried. My grandmother's death hit us hard. She was eighty-one, but none of us were ready for her to go. She was the matriarch of the family, and it was impossible to picture our lives without her. Losing her was also my first real experience with death. She was the closest person to me who had ever passed away. After watching her deteriorate, I made a promise to myself that I would never become a smoker.

That night, my relatives gathered at our house. We cried and laughed while sharing stories of my grandmother. One of my favorite memories was the night a few months earlier when my cousin Neda innocently asked Maman Soury if masturbation was considered a sin in Islam. I'd never seen my grandmother giggle so hard in my life. She couldn't get the words out to answer the question, and never managed a response.

The evening would only get more surreal as the hours inched later into the night. The gathering was coming to a close, and Neda was putting my brother to bed upstairs, away from the ruckus, when she noticed that my sister's bedroom smelled like smoke. She quickly alerted our parents, and my uncle went to investigate. By then, the entire second story of our house had filled with smoke. I remember hearing my uncle shout from upstairs for us to call 911 and to immediately evacuate the house. Minutes later, as my entire family stood on the sidewalk across the street, the fire department and paramedics showed up while flames shot through our roof. By the time the fire was under control, my sister's closet and our bathroom were burned to a crisp. According to the fire department, our whole house would have been up in flames if they'd been called fifteen minutes later.

The cause of the fire was a heater that had been poorly installed prior to our purchase of the house, and we slowly rebuilt the damage. But that night, we were all startled by the same thought as we watched the chaos outside our home. On any regular night, Samira and I would have been long asleep. We could have died of smoke inhalation. If my grandmother hadn't passed away that morning, we wouldn't have stayed up late with the rest of our family. It felt like the timing of her death wasn't by accident. It's possible she actually prevented another tragedy from befalling our family.

As the years rolled on, December 25 was never the same again for any of us. On the twentieth anniversary of my grandmother's death, Dayee Mohammad (her firstborn) died of complications from Parkinson's disease. It's hard to feel very festive on Christmas when our family has lost two loved ones on the holiday. When I'm in Northern California with my parents, we still start the day by opening gifts, and then we meet at my grandmother's grave to reminisce, exchange hugs and "I love yous," and tell her how much we miss her. Without fail, I think of her every time I stumble upon an episode of *Wheel of Fortune,* and wonder how the hell Pat Sajak and Vanna White haven't aged since the early nineties.

My problems may have seemed big to me in high school, but I wasn't dealing with arranged marriages to the wrong man or a love affair that would leave me ostracized from my entire family. Maman Soury didn't always make the most traditional decisions, but I wouldn't be here if it weren't for her struggles and hardships and the controversial paths she traveled down. My aunts, uncles, cousins, and I are all a product of the life she lived and the life she bravely chose not to live.

And though it was the furthest thing from any of our minds on the day she died, the loss of Maman Soury would also be a stumbling block in our immigration process. Just two years prior, my parents had gotten their divorce in hopes that my mom could secure a green card through her. There had been little movement on the application, and now there never would be.

December 25, 1994
I wish I'd been nicer to her. There were so many things
I wanted to tell her. I regret the way I treated her. I
want to write everything I remember about her now, so
when I read this I'll remember her. I remember her eyes

199

were green and beautiful, I remember she was a really good cook, I remember the little poems she would say, I remember how she played cards a lot, I remember her charm bracelet with all these golden hearts with each grandchild's name engraved on it. Most of all, I remember her smile. Sometimes I convinced myself that if I looked at her and smiled and she smiled back, things would be all right.

We sold our house and we'll be moving in about ten days. I can't really believe it. There's something about this home. It fits us. I love it. I really see it as protection, comfort. I promise one of these days I will buy this home back. I can't imagine waking up someplace else.

—Diary entry: September 28, 1997

Chapter Twelve

★

Home, Sweet Homeless

By my senior year of high school, I can say with total confidence, I'd seen my dad cry approximately one million times. I can't remember the first time he'd burst into tears in front of my siblings and me. Maybe it was at the end of *The Little Mermaid* when Ariel got legs and left her dad at the bottom of the ocean. (Seriously, WTF, Ariel? No dude is worth leaving your whole family for.) Or maybe it was one of the rare times he was able to talk about his brother even though he was still paralyzed by the grief of losing him. Or maybe it was one of the many times he looked at my mom and spontaneously declared how much he loved her. I couldn't tell you. But I can tell you the first time I saw him cry from shame. And I was the seventeen-year-old asshat who brought him to tears.

"I'm sorry," he mumbled in Farsi, his arms folded across his chest. "I'm sorry you don't want to live with us."

We were at Dayee Mehrdad's house, deep in the wooded hills of Saratoga, California. We were sitting across from each other on the bench of a bay window that looked out onto the long, steep driveway that led to their magnificent English Tudor. The room was large and well lit, and came with its own entrance and bathroom. It was the home's guest quarters, which doubled as my aunt Geneva's sewing room. It was also where I'd decided to run away to without my mom, dad, and brother. So what if I suffered from full-fledged panic attacks every time I drove our beat-up '88 Camry through the winding, narrow roads to my new temporary digs? My uncle's house was big and fancy, and I had a queen-size bed all to myself.

I'm sure that as my dad bawled his eyes out, I begged him to stop crying. I'm sure I apologized for being an ungrateful brat. I'm sure I hugged him and told him that I was proud of him and that he had nothing to be sorry for. But it's just as likely that I froze. I've always loved the fact that I have a dad who openly weeps. I'm glad a guy who wasn't void of emotion raised me. But in that moment, I wished he were one of those stereotypically cold, distant American dads or those stoic, strict Asian dads my friends always complained about. Those guys never cry, right?

But let's pause for a moment on my dad's red and puffy face, and cut to the events leading up to our provisional estrangement. It was three months earlier, the summer of 1997 to be exact, when my mom told me that we were putting our beloved home on the market. Soon our charming black-and-white house on Pinewood Drive would no longer belong to us. It would belong to people who could afford to live there. A family of American citizens or, at the very least, a family with green cards. A house with a swimming pool was not fit for the Saedis. We were a ragtag team of undocumented immigrants, and for us the American dream was more elusive than Banksy's true identity.

"But what about my collage?" I cried when my mom told me the news.

I had spent several painstaking weeks cutting out my favorite pictures from issues of *Us* magazine (back when it was still a respectable monthly publication). It had required at least two rolls of double-sided tape for the work of art to take up one massive wall of my bedroom. It was my pride and joy.

My older, college-educated cousin called it postmodern. I had no idea what that meant, but I totally agreed. And there was no way I could take apart every single picture and replicate the masterpiece in another bedroom. Izzy and I had also created a mural on another wall, and had taken great care to paint my blinds with the colors of the rainbow. I was hoping any potential buyers would be deterred by the thought of a fresh paint job and replacement blinds, but that wasn't the case.

My parents made it seem like they just wanted to downsize. With my sister out of the house, and with me a year away from college, they didn't need all the space. Why not live in a smaller, generic town house in a less expensive part

My postmodern collage.

of south San Jose that was twenty minutes farther from all my friends, my job, and my high school? But I knew what was really happening. Peninsula Luggage was floundering, and they could no longer afford our mortgage and my sister's college tuition.

Here's the thing. As an undocumented immigrant, you're screwed when it comes to filing for student loans to send your kids to college. Though it may have been tempting to commit a felony and covertly check the box that read "American citizen" on the application, my parents knew those financial aid peeps meant serious business. From what we'd been told, they'd conduct extensive background checks into our immigration status. A false claim would have been considered criminal activity and would have been grounds to deny our adjustment-of-status application and deport us. So instead, my parents tried to scrape together every penny to pay for my sister's college in full. Even though my dad worked as a waiter and bus driver to put himself through school, my parents hated the idea of my sister getting a job to help with her tuition. They wanted her to focus solely on her education. She would defy them and get a job anyway because, like me, she suffered from immigrant child guilt complex.

My parents had been self-employed for my entire life. They'd never had the benefits of a steady salary or paid vacation days. Their income was always unpredictable, and any time off or a lull in their business would impact how much money we had for bills and groceries each month. But luggage sales were only a small portion of Peninsula Luggage's cash flow. The main source of income was cocaine and illegal firearms. Not really, but I always liked to pretend the business was a front for the Persian mafia. Most of our profits actually came from luggage repairs. My parents had accounts with the various airlines and were hired to repair bags the airlines had damaged. Each day, my dad donned a white lab coat with his name, Ali, embroidered above the front pocket, and drove his giant red van to the San Jose and San Francisco airports to pick up suitcases in need of fixing. When his van wasn't filled with luggage, my friends and I would ride around in the back and slide up and down its slick floor anytime the car slowed to a stop. His employees loved working for him, and one even asked if my dad would be willing to sponsor him to get a green card. My dad had to break the embarrassing news that he couldn't, because he didn't have a green card, either. Despite his cheery disposition, I knew my dad hated what he did for a living.

"It's a thankless job," my dad always said of the business. "You're dealing with unhappy customers all the time."

But you'd never know this from the smile on his face when he got home around 9:00 p.m. and took off his white lab coat. The man was relentlessly upbeat and positive. "Don't worry, be happy" remains his mantra. Which was probably why I didn't realize the business was in a financial slump. Unbeknownst to me, after taking out an equity loan on our house to help pay my sister's tuition, my parents couldn't keep up with mortgage payments. If we didn't sell our house, the bank would put it in foreclosure.

I was eleven when we moved into our home on Pinewood Drive, and we would move out on my seventeenth birthday. In hindsight, I was a psycho bitch throughout the ordeal. We'd be moving into the sixth house we'd lived in since we arrived in America, while my high school friends continued to occupy their childhood homes. They each had walls in their houses that documented their height and growth spurts, beginning with the year they could stand on two feet. They had neighborhood cookouts, and could paint and decorate the walls of their bedrooms with every assurance that they'd never have to pack their bags and leave. We never had that sense of security. We bounced around from house to house, usually opting for the more affordable and less desirable parts of town. Anytime we had money trouble, my parents would say we were rich in love. And we were. But love doesn't pay the mortgage. And it also doesn't buy a colorful collection of Doc Martens.

Six years was the longest we'd lived in any house, and I had become hopelessly attached to our San Jose neighborhood. I loved that we lived within rollerblading distance of a local Japanese market that sold candy with edible wrappers. We still lived off the beaten path, but Pinewood Drive was much closer to my friends and school than the San Jose locales my parents were now considering. As pissed off as I was at my baba and maman for putting our house on the market, I also sympathized with their predicament. I didn't want them to lose any more sleep over our financial problems.

But once we officially sold our house and moving day came around, I was inconsolable. On the inside of my closet door, I wrote an epic poem to the new owners telling them the house would always belong to *me:*

PINEWOOD

Money means nothing to me.
Objects make me smile for a second.
But this home I can't let go of.
These walls, I've cried for.

I've had screaming fights in this bedroom.
I've danced crazy all alone.
I've stayed up all night with loved ones.
I've talked on the phone with boys I've loved.

This has been my shelter from the storm.
This is where I wrote my poetry.
This is where I've wanted to die.
These are my memories you've taken from me.

So you can paint over my pictures,
erase these bitter words.
But one thing won't change,
the life that's been spent.

This home is a part of me,
And I'm a part of this house.
You can sleep here if you like.
You can buy it with your money.

But my music lingers.
These walls will miss my family's voice.
So this place you call home,
Will always belong to me.

One day I'll buy it back.

I like to imagine the new family was so touched by my poignant words that they decided not to paint over them. Perhaps they could tell that whoever wrote it would be a writer someday and that eventually the poem would be worth more than the house. Honestly, I wouldn't be surprised if they leave me the place in their will.

October 6, 1997
My birthday is on Friday. The death day. The day we leave. My last few days of being sixteen, and living in this house. Why is this life so twisted and broken? Even though I shouldn't, part of me blames my parents.

I know they are worse off than I am. But I know they
want to get out of here. I hate every happy naïve
stupid person. And I hate feeling sorry for myself. And
I hate being in this room. These walls are mocking me,
laughing at my tears . . .

After we sold our house, we were officially homeless. We
hadn't found another place to live and had to regress back
to our old fobby selves and shack up with relatives. My parents opted to move in with my aunt and uncle in their modest
three-bedroom house in Cupertino. Even though their place
was walking distance to my high school, I decided that I didn't
want to be in such tight quarters. Instead, I would move in
with Dayee Mehrdad. Both his kids were out of the house. Of
course he and my aunt would *love* the idea of a teenager suddenly living with them. They had enough room. They weren't
just rich in love; they were rich in money. Plus, my aunt Geneva totally dug me. She never learned to speak Farsi, and I
would hang out with her at all our family parties and talk
Oscar predictions. There was a good chance that after I'd lived
with them for a few days, they would beg my parents to allow
them to adopt me . . . and then I'd get a green card in no time.

I lasted two days at my uncle's house. My parents were a
mere five miles away, but it felt like they were on the other
side of the world. I worried that I had created an unbridge-
able divide by rejecting them and choosing my uncle, with
his elegant home in the promised land of Saratoga. I cried
myself to sleep from loneliness. It wasn't my aunt and uncle's

fault. Their generosity over the years could fill up this entire book, but their lives functioned differently from those of my parents. They didn't have kids in the house and were used to doing their own thing. They slept in separate bedrooms because my uncle's snoring was so loud it was inhumane. They also didn't eat dinner together, because my uncle's dining preferences still included eating at midnight with his gin martini and then going straight to bed.

The day I arrived at my uncle's house, he gave me a hundred dollars to buy my own groceries. He explained that they didn't really cook and usually fended for themselves for dinner. I tried to turn down the money (*taarof*!), but he wouldn't let me. I didn't tell him that I didn't know how to cook and that I'd never bought my own groceries. Instead, I hoped they wouldn't judge me when I dined on Noodle Roni like the peasant that I was.

Maybe it was the thought of home-cooked Persian meals that lured me to my aunt's house in Cupertino. Or the fact that eight-year-old Kia and I were inseparable, and it felt wrong to abandon him. Or that in two days, I hadn't figured out how to get the hot water to work in my uncle's bathroom and that no form of deodorant would mask the stench of my body odor. No, I'm pretty sure what completely did me in was my dad, sitting on that windowsill, apologizing for selling our house and for the mess that we were now in. And then, through his tears, he apologized for failing me.

But he'd never failed me.

When my mom and dad had left behind their entire country to give me a better life, they didn't write angsty poetry on the walls before they made their departure. They just left . . . knowing they might never return. Not to my grandfathers' graves or my mother's childhood home or the site of their first official date. If they could be that resilient, then I could move to a different part of San Jose without making such a giant fuss about it.

"I don't want to stay with Dayee anymore. I want to live at Khaleh's house with you guys," I told my dad, now through my own tears.

My declaration to end our forty-eight-hour estrangement didn't slow down my dad's crying, but I could tell his emotions had taken on a different form. After months, he'd finally been absolved of his guilt. I only wish I'd told him sooner that he had nothing to feel guilty about. I packed up my suitcase and explained to my uncle that I felt bad about leaving my parents. I tried to give him the grocery money back, but in typical Persian-uncle form, he refused it.

That night, I went to sleep in a cozy bed at my aunt's house, while my parents slept on the floor of the same bedroom. One more sacrifice in a string of many. As I looked down at my mom and dad, it dawned on me that a house doesn't make a home without the people who live inside it. As cheesy as it sounded at the time, my mom and dad were right: crammed in that tiny bedroom together, we were still rich in love.

A month later, we moved into the Camden Village town houses right off the Camden exit on Highway 85 South. I didn't complain about the long drive to school, or the fact that we had to get bunk beds for my room so that my sister would have a place to sleep when she came home from college. I would even go on to make another collage. If I had to name the piece, I'd call it:

Resilience.

FREQUENTLY ASKED QUESTION #6
Why the hell is it the year 1396 in Iran?

Upon the publication of this book in 2018, it's 1396 in Iran. Crazy, right? There is a method to this madness. While the United States is on the Gregorian calendar, Iran uses the Solar Hijri calendar. According to the Solar Hijri, the starting day of the year aligns with the vernal equinox, which is why Eid (Persian New Year) is always at the start of spring. The holiday is usually a great excuse for Iranians to throw parties, shower their children with crisp dolla dolla bills, and eat one of our favorite traditional dishes: sabzi polo and mahi (rice with fresh herbs and fish).

The country officially switched to the Solar Hijri calendar in 1925, under the Pahlavi dynasty. They also coordinated the beginning of the calendar with the pilgrimage of the Prophet Muhammad from Mecca to Medina in 622 CE. And thus, the year suddenly went from 1925 to 1303. To make matters even more confusing, the origin of the calendar was changed again in 1976. The shah decided to change the starting point from Muhammad's spiritual journey to the beginning of Cyrus the Great's reign. And thus the year suddenly went from 1355 to 2535.

After the Islamic Revolution, the origin date reverted back to Muhammad's pilgrimage. Iranians are basically time travelers. One may think all of these calendar changes would have no impact on me since I live in America, but I discovered later in life that I have a completely different birth date from the one I'd been told by my parents. All of my legal documents said that I was born on September 22, 1980, but it turns out that date is entirely false. I was actually born in October, but in Iran that would have meant waiting an entire year to start school and my parents didn't want me to be one of the oldest kids in the class. They fudged the dates on my birth certificate so that I wouldn't be held back for a year. Then we moved to America and the birth-date fraud became completely irrelevant. As a child, I celebrated my birthday on September 22, but my parents eventually revealed to me that I was born on October 10. This fact absolutely delighted me when I was a kid. I had two birthdays! What could be better than that?

But then, as a teenager, I got really into zodiac signs and concluded that it was so much cooler to be a Libra than a boring Virgo. I decided I would begin to celebrate my birthday on October 10 instead. The date of my birth got even more confusing when my dad accidentally filled out an immigration document incorrectly and suddenly I was born on September 21. And then my mom dropped another bomb. She told me I was either born on the tenth or the eleventh of October.

"WHAAAAT?" was my general response.

My mom, frustrated, finally responded that I was

born on "the twentieth of Mehr in 1359," according to the Iranian calendar. I think we can all agree that I look extremely good for being 659 years old. Luckily, the Internet was finally around, so I could convert the twentieth of Mehr in 1359 to the exact date on the US calendar. The website revealed I was actually born on . . . drumroll, please . . . October 12, 1980. So I didn't know my actual birthdate until I was around twenty years old.

To complicate matters even further, when I finally received my green card, they accidentally printed my birthday as September 21, 1982 (the year we arrived in the United States—not the year I was actually born). I guess I didn't mind suddenly being two years younger . . . though I once got turned away from a bar when I was of legal drinking age because the bouncer saw the date of birth on my green card and told me I wasn't old enough to come in.

Did you get all of that?

Currently, as far as the government and my driver's license are concerned, I was born on September 21, 1980 . . . even though I was still resting comfortably inside my mom's womb that day.

I wanted to go so bad. I wanted to wear my dress and look pretty, and I wanted him to think I was beautiful. I told my mom I wanted him to feel as bad as I feel, but she said no guy in this world will come close to feeling what I feel right now, because they don't feel things like that. Evan can't feel.

—Diary entry: April 22, 1997

Chapter Thirteen

◆ ★ ◆

Sex, Prom, and Other Catastrophes

Every morning when my dad dropped me off at school, he left me with the same piece of advice. As I stepped out of the car and mentally prepared myself for another potentially traumatic day of high school, he would say, "Be nice to the boys!"

I can still hear his upbeat foreign accent advising me to be my best self around the opposite sex. I don't know whether he was just trying to be facetious or if he actually worried that I walked around campus acting like a raving lunatic. The Saedi/Sanjideh women can be fiery and irrational and difficult to please. Even though I was a ball of insecurity, I came from a long line of women with high expectations and high standards for other people. I usually laughed off my dad's advice, but I wanted to tell him that he had it all wrong. It was the boys who needed to be nice to me. I was not the problem when it came to my lifelong relationship dry spell. Guys weren't into me. I was the girl in my clique whom dudes sought out when they had a crush on another girl and needed advice on how to win her over. I usually found myself in the friend zone right away. I was the girl who had never even French-kissed a boy. There were girls in my senior class who'd been having sex for most of high school, and I hadn't even felt a guy's tongue inside my mouth. My lack of experience was a source of shame and the root of all my insecurities. Sixteen was far too old to have never been kissed. Somewhere along the way, my libido had fallen behind the curve. But I kept telling myself that my dating life was about to take a turn for the better. All this time, I'd never been kissed, because I was meant to be kissed at . . .

PROM.

My friends and I had rejected most of the societal norms of high school, but we still bought into the iconic powers of formal dances. Even the potheads who hung out at Rainbow Park entertained the idea of trading in their withered thermal shirts for a tux or a Jessica McClintock ball gown to go to prom. And now that we were juniors, we didn't have to rely on upperclassmen to take us as their dates. It was our time. We were finally going to have our own prom.

In a small clique of six girls, there was a high probability that we'd all go to the dance. Hopefully, a few of us would snag dates and the rest of us could go stag together. I had no qualms about going dateless, as long as I had friends who were also happy to treat the event like a very fancy girls' night out. Together, we could hitch a ride in someone's limo and form our own little dance circle. I considered myself an independent woman. I didn't need a guy to make me happy (even though every single diary entry will beg to differ). But then something awful happened. Within weeks, everyone in my clique found a date to prom except me. It didn't matter if I wanted to be a young Gloria Steinem. I wasn't insane. There was no way I was going to go stag to prom without a stag posse.

When spring break rolled around just a couple of weeks before the dance and I still didn't have a date, I resigned myself to the fact that I wouldn't be going . . . and then I spotted my dream dress hanging on a rack at Macy's. My friend Rebecca and I had kicked off the first day of break by hitting up the mall together, and that's when I saw the gown in all its glory. I'd seen it before at Jessica McClintock, but they didn't carry it in my size and eventually sold out of the dress. But now here it was, and with a few alterations, it would fit me perfectly.

I still love everything about that dress (see my photo with Neda on page 156). It was my favorite shade of lavender. The material was velvet—which we've already established was quite popular in the nineties. It was a sleeveless tank dress that hugged my hips, but the back of the gown was what sealed the deal for me. It was mostly backless, with excess material that drooped just above my waist. I promptly took my mom to Macy's and she agreed that the dress was made for me, but there was one condition on her part. She would buy it for me *only if* I asked Evan Parker to prom. My mom was essentially blackmailing me into being a good feminist and following my heart.

You remember Evan Parker, right? The stoner boy I was madly in love with. I don't think my mom knew about his recreational drug use, or she wouldn't have urged me to take a leap of faith and ask him out. I knew he didn't have a date. I also knew that he was one of the few guys at school who weren't really into prom in the first place. I couldn't believe my mom was encouraging me to be so ballsy. She was even more of a badass than I'd previously thought. She wanted me to be the kind of girl who went after what I wanted, and I wasn't about to let her down. Plus, I *really* wanted that dress. If prom didn't work out, I could always wear it to a family wedding.

She purchased the dress, and as soon as we got home, I mustered all my courage and dialed Evan's phone number. It wasn't that unusual for me to call him. We'd been phone buddies the previous summer, and ten days of spring break would feel like an eternity away from him. His mom answered and put him on the phone.

I was too nervous to make much small talk. We discussed our plans over break, and then I dropped the prom bomb. I tried to keep it casual and prefaced the question by saying that I knew dances weren't his cup of tea . . . but would he like to go to prom with me? There was a brief pause. And then he said, "Getting dressed up and going to dances isn't really my thing, but I'd go with you, because you're cool."

Evan Parker thought I was cool. My life almost felt complete.

There was one slight catch. Prom was expensive, and he'd have to ask his mom if he could have the money. Since I was a woman of the nineties, I offered to pay for the tickets, but he refused. Plus, it still wouldn't cover the cost of renting a tux. He promised he would ask his mom about his financial situation, and then he'd get back to me. I hung up the phone feeling empowered. I had found the dress, and I had called the guy and asked him to be my date. I would be joining my friends in their limo with Evan Freaking Parker. There was no way his mom wouldn't give him the proper funds to go to *prom*. How could she resist getting photos of her son in a bow tie?

What followed was an agonizing week of waiting for Evan to call me back to say that, yes, he was going to prom with me. Luckily, I had Rebecca to distract me. She was going to the dance with a close guy friend who was madly in love with her, but during that brief era in our lives, it didn't matter that boys commonly fell at the feet of Rebecca's Amazonian body. It all seemed secondary to the fact that her family was in crisis. Her dad had recently moved out of their house, and Rebecca was reeling from her parents' sudden divorce. So I helped distract her, too. We spent every single day together and let ourselves obsess over how much fun prom would be once Evan agreed to be my date. I was grateful to spend the days outside the house with her. Back when there weren't cell phones, you weren't waiting by the phone by default. With Rebecca driving us to the beach in Santa Cruz during the day or to downtown San Jose to hang out at night, I could distract myself from Evan, and the fact that I still hadn't heard from him. My heart would immediately race the moment I came home and saw the red blinking light of my answering machine. I'd even recorded an outgoing message with Evan in mind. When my machine picked up, you heard the Doors singing "Hello, I love you, won't you tell me your name," followed by the *beep*. But the entire week passed and there were no messages from Evan.

The Monday back at school, Evan approached me in the morning and broke the news that he'd spoken to his mom and she told him that the dance was too expensive. I didn't know why it had taken him an entire week to give me the answer. It would have been so much easier to get bad news over the phone than in person. I managed to smile and say that I understood, but my dreams had just died a slow and torturous death. I knew the money dilemma was just an excuse. If Evan Parker *liked* me, if he really wanted to go to prom with me, he would have found a way to make it happen. He would have sold his body to science to spend the most memorable night of our lives together.

It wasn't just the rejection that upset me. It was the fact that all my friends would be at prom without me. They would get their hair and makeup done together. They'd put on fancy dresses, and everyone's parents would be there taking photographs of them and their dates. They'd get in a limo and eat a fancy dinner, and then go to the dance. They'd make lifelong memories, and I wouldn't be included in any of them. One of the reasons my parents had left a war-torn country to bring me to America, after all, was so that I could enjoy all the perks and freedoms that other American teenagers were allowed to experience. There was no such thing as prom in Iran, and there would be no such thing as prom for me, either. The dance was just days away. There was no chance I'd find another date in time, and I didn't want to be there with anyone who wasn't Evan. My perfect dress would just gather dust in the closet. I was, in a word, heartbroken.

Luckily, while I was having an emotional meltdown in third period, Rebecca suggested we ditch the rest of the day at school and walk home. I was grateful she was willing to cut class so that Evan wouldn't learn that he'd turned me into a blubbering wreck. Saving face was all I had left. I cursed all men through my tears. As we waited at a crosswalk for the light to change, Rebecca gently replied, "At least you still have faith in your dad. I can't even say that anymore." There we were, two girls from vastly different backgrounds and belief systems, born on opposite sides of the globe, and yet, in that moment, none of that mattered. We understood each other completely. I felt her pain as much as she felt mine.

Aside from Rebecca, two other heroes emerged from this story: my maman and Samira. There was no one who knew how to console me like my mom. Maybe she was just tired of hearing the Wallflowers album on repeat on my stereo, but she sat with me in my room for hours and tried to tell me that in a few years Evan Parker would be nothing but a distant memory. I didn't understand how she'd gotten so wise about relationships. She'd never even dated before she married my dad.

"I wish I had never asked him," I told my mom.

Her response has stayed with me ever since.

"It's always better to put yourself out there. Sometimes you'll hear no, but you'll never hear yes, either, unless you ask."

She was right, I thought. At least I tried. At least I would never have to look back and wonder if things could have gone differently if I'd only asked Evan to the dance. I'd always known that my mom and I had completely different upbringings. Even though the Iran she knew as a teenager used to be more progressive, dating wasn't as widely accepted as it was in America. My mom had distant crushes and a few experiences with unrequited love, but there was no way she knew *exactly* what I was feeling. Immigrant kids often feel like their parents will never understand what it's like to be a teenager in the States. They'll never fully comprehend what it's like to bounce back and forth between two worlds and two cultures without offending either side. But it was then that I understood one of my mom's greatest virtues: her capacity for empathy. She didn't have to know my pain in order to feel it. Despite a cultural chasm that would exist between us no matter how long we lived in America, I'd never felt more connected to her.

My parents also knew that they had to buoy me up on prom night. There was no way I could be crying into a tub of ice cream at home. I would have to forge my own memories of that weekend that didn't include hating myself and wondering every second what my friends were doing. I'm so grateful that social media didn't exist back then. My fragile heart would not have survived seeing up-to-the-minute photos of my friends and classmates on Facebook or Instagram or Snapchat. I would have had to stick my iPhone in a bag of rice from all the water damage it would have incurred from my tears. Luckily, my parents hatched a last-minute plan. They rented a hotel room in Santa Cruz, and my sister drove down from college to spend the weekend there with me. She was most likely missing some big college party, but I was so glad she was willing to drop everything to make sure a stint in the psych ward wasn't on the horizon for me.

I wouldn't trade those two days with my sister for anything in the world. Her weekends home were always divided between visits with her high school friends and our cousins and other relatives. It was rare that we got forty-eight uninterrupted hours together. We went to the beach and out to brunch and dinner. After much discussion, we agreed that Evan Parker wasn't good enough for me anyway. While all my friends were doing the running man to Snoop Dogg, I was smoking pot with my sister in a hotel room and going to see *Romy and Michele's High School Reunion* in the theaters—arguably one of the best movies ever made. (That is *not* hyperbole.)

I'm warning you now, young readers. Soak up the time you have with your siblings. The years will inevitably go by and you will get older. You may live far away from each other. You will get married and have kids and responsibilities that make it hard to talk on the phone daily or see each other very often. That weekend with my sister was so much more meaningful than a night with a stoner boy who thought I was "cool." It turned out that Evan Parker, and his strict mom, and his nonexistent finances culminated in some of my most pivotal memories from high school. Plus, my sister pointed out one very important detail that helped me emerge from the bell jar: senior prom was the only prom that *really* mattered.

Cut to one year later.

Evan was now a Ghost of High School Past. He'd left Lynbrook for a program called "middle college," where high school seniors could take classes at the local community college, and his absence finally allowed me to focus on other guys.

Enter my friend Slash. Once he came into the picture, I finally stumbled on what had been eluding me through my teen years: *mutual* attraction. Slash (fake name inspired by his love for the band Guns N' Roses) and I had been buddies for most of high school. I never actually considered him as a romantic prospect, because of one fatal flaw. He was *too* tall.

Way too tall. More than a foot taller than me. I thought I was destined for short men. We would look awkward together. How would we even be able to kiss when my face barely went up to his chest? Slash was also categorically eccentric, and a bit of a nerd. He was really into death metal, so he usually came to school dressed head to toe in black. He'd grown out his silky brown hair so that it reached his lower back and had sideburns that took up half his face.

Slash and I had a knack for flirtatious banter, but part of the reason I never considered him boyfriend material was that he *always* had a girlfriend. He usually dated underclassmen with Alanis Morissette–style hair and an affinity for grunge attire. By then, after a year of using my employee discount at the Gap, my wardrobe bore a striking resemblance to that of Ali MacGraw in *Love Story*. I never thought I was his type, but ours was a "right in front of me the whole time" kind of romance. By the end of senior year, he was finally single, and our friendship evolved into full-fledged coupledom.

Surprisingly, my parents didn't take issue with our relationship even though Slash was the furthest thing from all the nice, respectable Persian men in our family. The only Iranian guys I knew were related to me, and anytime I met one who wasn't, I instantly felt a familial connection. The physical attraction was nonexistent. Luckily, my parents weren't all that fazed by Slash's long hair and black metal T-shirts with images of slaughtered, naked women. My dad even tried to impress him by telling him that my parents had seen Ozzy Osbourne in concert.

"Really?" Slash asked.

"Yeah," my dad answered. "He was onstage with all his brothers and sisters."

"Those were the *Osmonds*!" my mom corrected.

Despite my dad confusing Donny Osmond for Ozzy Osbourne, he and Slash were still able to bond over bands like Pink Floyd and Jethro Tull. It also helped that Slash was polite and friendly, and nicknamed me *khoshkeleh,* which is Farsi for "pretty one."

Mostly, I was happy that I was finally getting some experience under my belt before graduation. My first kiss with Slash was relatively uneventful. I was hanging out in his room, like I often did, listening to him play bass. Eventually, he moved to the bed and kissed me without much warning. I froze. I wasn't really sure what to do. Before I could kiss him back, he was on top of me, and I tried to follow his lead. It wasn't by any means an awful kiss, but I told myself that it would get better. Afterward, he walked me to the door, and we said good night. I promptly ran to Izzy's house, which was just across the street, and shared the momentous news. I was no longer a supervirgin. I was *just* a virgin. More important, my well-timed relationship with Slash meant I had a date to senior prom.

I'd already worn my lavender gown to a winter formal, so for prom I opted for a black-and-white lace dress that I'd spotted in the window at Bebe. It had enough Goth influences to fit with Slash's aesthetic, but it still felt classic and timeless. I wasn't even the slightest bit embarrassed that he opted for a maroon tux, a top hat, a cape, and a cane. My parents were most likely confused by his outfit choice, but they seemed to accept the fact that Slash had a unique look and personality. And I did, too. I realized that I didn't want boring in my life, and that a cape and top hat were so much more interesting than the black-and-white tuxedo every other guy was wearing. I was beginning to shed my insecurities. I cared less about what everyone else at our high school thought of me. I was proud to be Slash's girlfriend, and once prom ended, we would be inseparable through the last weeks of school and all our graduation festivities. I would still be an illegal immigrant, but at least now I was one with an American boyfriend and a high school diploma.

My family and me at my high school graduation.

With college on the horizon, part of me wondered if it was a mistake for us to try to stay together, but Slash was such a great boyfriend, and I couldn't imagine finding anyone else who'd be interested in me. He was sentimental and romantic. At seventeen, his favorite thing to do was to take me to four-star restaurants throughout Silicon Valley. We dined on fondue and freshly made pasta. He also had this adorable habit of kissing my hand—probably because he was into knights and swords—and referred to women as "milady."

I felt like I was being wined and dined, but that didn't change the fact that I was petrified at the thought of consummating our relationship. To be fair, I was still getting used to French-kissing and having my boobs fondled. We'd been dating for only a few months, but I also couldn't imagine losing my virginity to anyone else. So as college approached, I decided that I couldn't live without Slash. We agreed to stay together, but dates to fancy restaurants, thoughtful gifts, and a constant refrain of sweet nothings didn't allay what had now become my irrational fear about sex. "What am I so afraid of?" I wondered.

The answer was simple. The answer was my parents. Most of my friends' parents had come of age in the era of free love, but my maman and baba had totally missed out on the sexual revolution. While they grew up in a more progressive Iran before the Islamic Revolution, the country was still conservative when it came to matters of sex, and Persian women were especially modest on the topic of sexuality. Before my mom was married, she was strolling around Tehran with her female cousin. A convertible full of handsome young men slowed down next to them, and a flirtation ensued. The guys got out of the car and exchanged phone numbers with my mom and her cousin. But unbeknownst to them, the entire interaction was witnessed by one of my dayee Shahrdad's friends. When my uncle heard secondhand that my mom was flirting with guys in the neighborhood, he was quick to confront her. She admitted it was true, and he reacted by promptly slapping her across the face, which is almost comical, because my whole life I'd describe my uncle as a total softie who wouldn't hurt a fly. After that experience, she wasn't all that interested in pursuing any secret relationships, which was why marriage was her first real attempt at dating.

My mom's upbringing in Iran seemed to permeate other areas of her life in America. Even when my sister and I were teenagers, she seemed shy about changing her clothes in front of us. Her modesty totally rubbed off on me. I became quite the ninja when it came to undressing in our high school locker room, developing strategies to change my clothes so that no one would actually have to see me naked. My underwear always came on and off beneath the shield of a towel. I'd often clasp my bra on over my towel, and then pull the towel down so that no one could get a good look at my tiny boobs.

My parents didn't talk to us in depth about sex, except to tell us that we were too young to be having it and that it was all boys wanted. I knew that my dad was a lothario before he met my mother, and that my mom had never had sex with anyone besides him. I also sensed that she resented this detail about their past. If the present could remain unchanged, then she would have gladly gone back in time to get more action. My mom even told me that she was a believer in premarital sex. Even though she couldn't actually fathom the idea of her daughters having sex until we were well into our twenties, she did not want us to wait until we were married to do it. That didn't mean she wanted us to throw ourselves at random men, but she hoped we'd test-drive a few before settling down. It was a truly feminist approach to sex, and when my mom explained it to me, I thought she was the coolest person ever.

Slash and I continued to date, off and on, for the next year. *And* we finally had sex, the summer after my freshman year in college. I'd made plans to stay over at his apartment and told my parents that I was staying the night with Izzy. I wore matching undergarments and slathered my legs in shimmery lotion. I was ready to throw my hymen an epic good-bye party. We started the night off by going to the movies, and when we got back to his place, I implied that I was "tired" so Slash and I could say good night to his roommates and retire to his bedroom. But instead of joining me, he opted to stay up and play video games with his buddies. I remember lying in his bed, tossing and turning, wondering why he'd lacked the ability to read my mind. A couple hours later, he returned to his room and complained that his stomach hurt.

I was furious. We got into a huge argument, and he admitted that there'd been too much buildup to consummating our relationship. He was even more nervous than I was at this point. Naturally, I found his fears and insecurities totally irresistible, and the night ended in careful, slow, and awkward sex. I was glad I was with someone I loved, but it turned out that nothing about it was as scary as I'd imagined. All I could think after it was over was that sex was wildly overrated.

But I was still afraid that my parents would be angry or ashamed of me if they found out I was no longer a virgin. I didn't have any intention of telling them, but keeping it from them also felt weirdly dishonest. About a month later, my mom found out anyway. My parents, Kia, and I had taken a weekend trip to Carmel, a quaint beach town about ninety minutes away from our house. We sat down for lunch, and my brother and dad left the table to use the bathroom. It was during this five-minute window that my mom asked me if there was anything Slash and I had done that she should know about.

I was so stunned that I didn't know how to respond, but the answer was written all over my face. My mom went pale. She had brought it up so casually because she never expected the answer to be yes. What followed was the most uncomfortable lunch of my entire life. My dad and brother had no idea what had happened, but my mom and I were both on the verge of passing out.

The next day, my mom gave me a stern lecture that

confirmed my fears that she was ashamed of me. She wanted to make sure that Slash and I were using condoms, and that I was being careful. Not just about pregnancy, but about my feelings, too. Sex wasn't something to be taken lightly. She made it clear that she thought I was too young, and that she wasn't happy about this new development in my love life. Though I knew my parents were generally more traditional about sex, I was still surprised by how distraught she seemed during this conversation. She was the same woman who had condoned premarital sex. Not to mention, I was two months shy of turning nineteen—the age she was when she married my dad. What happened to her empathy?

September 5, 1999
Kia and Baba went to the bathroom and Maman picked that moment to ask if Slash and I had had sex. Of course like I knew I would, I turned beet red. I was so mortified that it was obvious what the answer to her question was. I could tell she was extremely disturbed although she tried not to show it. She was mostly upset that I hadn't told her, but I still wish she hadn't found out. She looks at me different now. She thinks I'm too young and the whole pregnancy issue makes her nervous. I understand where she's coming from, but the way she acted nearly devalued the experience of not sex, but making love.*

---

*If there's one thing that embarrasses me in this book, it's my use of "making love" in this diary entry.

Two months later, when I was back at college, our relationship hit a wall. I didn't want to admit it at first, but I could sense that Slash was acting distant. "Are you going to break up with me?" I asked one night, over the phone.

"I don't know . . . ," he said.

"Do you still love me?" I said, the fear surfacing in my voice.

"No . . ."

I got off the phone as quickly as I could. Even though it was midnight, I dialed my mom in tears and told her that Slash had said he didn't love me anymore.

"What do I do?" I asked, hyperventilating.

"Sara *joon*,"* my mom replied, "why would you even want to make things work with someone who says they don't love you?"

Once again, my mom had proven she was the second coming of Confucius. She was right. Why would I want to be with someone who didn't love me? Before I'd called her, I was already trying to figure out how to convince Slash that we were meant to be, but my mom had given me the clarity that I needed. The moment Slash answered no when I asked if he still loved me, the relationship was over.

My mom remained my rock the way she always had through my romantic dramas, but most important, she never again made me feel ashamed or less than for sleeping with Slash. I was worried I'd get a lecture about how it wasn't

---

Joon, a term of endearment in Farsi, means "dear."

worth having sex with a boy if I couldn't even trust him with my heart, but my maman didn't pass any judgment. From that day forward, as more guys came into my life that didn't seem to deserve my love or return my affection, I simply reminded myself of my mom's advice. Why would I want to make things work with anyone who didn't love me? Why would anyone?

I tried to keep busy, but I kept crying. I fell asleep for an hour. But I thought I was going to puke. I tried to barf in the bathroom, but it didn't work. It was so awful. I talked to my parents and things are good now, but that day really messed up my way of thinking about things. I think my parents are miserable. And I think they have a lot of ill feelings toward me. I don't know about having kids. I feel like more of a burden and I don't trust my parents as much as I used to.

—Diary entry: March 29, 1998

Chapter Fourteen

◆ ★ ◆

Illegal Immigrant Problems

My light blue corduroy pants that I'd proudly purchased with my 50 percent employee discount at the Gap were ruined forever. Hot drips of my café mocha spilled onto my thighs, but I was crying too hard to hold the cup still as my dad weaved through traffic on 280, right past the Winchester Mystery House, the only recognizable San Jose landmark and one that I had never visited in the fifteen years we lived in the city. Sarah Winchester was famously convinced that spirits cursed her family and that if she kept building staircases that led to nothing, the confused ghosts wouldn't kill her. Right about then, I was considering doing the same thing to our town house so my parents wouldn't be able to hunt me down and end my short life.

"Where are you taking me?" I asked, not recognizing the route we were on as the one that normally got us home.

"Mebareemet ghabrestoon," my mom responded drily. This directly translates to "We're taking you to the cemetery." I didn't know it at the time, but this is an Iranian saying used when someone complains about having to go somewhere. I just thought it meant my parents were going to murder me.

There were only two other things I was able to process during that tumultuous drive. My parents were in the throes of a nervous breakdown, and *I* had driven them to the edge of insanity. If my dad slowed down the car to shove me out of it, the cops probably would have deemed it a fair punishment.

The car ride that day in March is forever imprinted in my mind as the worst fight I've ever had with my parents. They'd taken me out of school for the day to deal with immigration paperwork, but as the end of my senior year was approaching, all I wanted to do was hang out with my friends; flirt with Slash, who was then on the precipice of becoming my boyfriend; and head over to Izzy's after school to gossip about our friends and potential love interests. Our favorite pastime was playing a game we'd invented called Random. We'd load her five-disc CD player with our favorite albums and treat it like an oracle. We'd ask questions about our future ("Is Slash into me?"), then hit the "random" button on her stereo system. Whatever song played would be the answer to the question. But instead of learning what the future held, I'd been dragged to downtown San Jose so my parents could fill out paperwork with our immigration lawyer.

I didn't care if we were supposedly nearing the end of our legalization nightmare. We were always supposedly nearing the end of our legalization nightmare. I wanted to be a normal teenager. I was sick to death of visits to the INS that required standing in lines that made the DMV look like a spa day. Just renewing my employment authorization card required waiting outside at 6:00 a.m. for the doors to open three hours later. Most teenagers camped out for concert tickets, but I had to camp out so that I could continue to legally work in the country. Stupidly, I always thought the agents would be nicer to me than other immigrants, because at least I spoke perfect English. But they treated me with the same disdain they did everyone else who passed through the metal detectors, all of us equally confused by their rules and their paperwork that always seemed to be missing some important piece of the required file. There was no worse feeling of defeat than waiting at the INS for five-plus hours, only to be turned away for not presenting the proper paperwork that you could have sworn you'd never even received in the mail. I had reached my boiling point. I officially had illegal immigrant fatigue, and it had caused the most dramatic family rift I'd ever experienced.

That particular day, I threw a fit when it looked like our dealings at our lawyer's office would take longer than expected and I wouldn't get to hang out at Izzy's. By then,

I'd gotten used to bitching under my breath when it came to our immigration issues, only to have my parents frantically apologize for the messy state of affairs. But this time, something snapped inside of them. All the uncomfortable and vicious fights I'd witnessed between my American friends and their parents suddenly seemed like child's play. I couldn't bite my tongue or stop myself from talking back. I was acting like every rude teenager I'd been secretly horrified by.

Years of frustration and stress were spilling over on both sides. On my parents' end, they couldn't understand why I was making an already challenging situation worse. On my end, I realized something I'd never quite verbalized before: this had nothing to do with me. It was their fault. Why didn't they immediately apply for political asylum? Why didn't my mom bite the bullet and enter into a fake marriage to get us green cards faster? Why did they trust incompetent lawyers who steered us in the wrong direction, just because *those* lawyers were Iranian? I should have been cursing the system, but my mom and dad were much more tangible scapegoats. But they no longer had it in them to quietly take the blame and apologize for inconveniencing my life. For once, they decided to fight back.

The most disturbing part of our argument in the car that day was the moment my dad declared that he hated his life. Looking back, I know he didn't mean it at all. It was a comment he made out of sheer exhaustion and anger. This was still the man whose motto was "Don't worry, be happy." Nothing seemed to get under his skin. But hearing him say that he hated his life brought on a sobering realization for me: my parents were *human*. They had their own disappointments and regrets. Over the years, I had never considered their happiness. It was just a given. Of course they were happy. They had three healthy children who adored them (most of the time). What more could they want in the world? The thought of them waking up feeling sad or miserable made me sick to my stomach.

After years of paperwork, lawyers' fees, and an unwanted divorce, my parents were finally falling to pieces. If anyone out there thinks that undocumented immigrants are privately high-fiving each other and throwing backyard barbecues to celebrate their free ride in America, let me assure you that is not the case. What followed our blowup were heartfelt apologies on my end and my parents' end, but we had no idea that our immigration status was about to get far more complicated and scary. The worst was yet to come.

In June of that same year, my sister was about to turn twenty-one. This meant she could drink legally and go to bars. It also meant she could buy me alcohol upon request, and that we looked enough alike that I could use her ID to go to bars myself if I wanted. She was as excited as any warm-blooded alcohol-loving American would be. And that's partially why my parents had decided not to tell her that turning twenty-one also meant that she would no longer be allowed to get a green card through the application we'd filed with my uncle as our sponsor. This is what the INS calls "aging out." It's a term used when an accompanying child on an application turns twenty-one before the case has been approved. That means the child can no longer be granted permanent residency as part of their parents' application. We'd filed to get a green card through my uncle in 1985, and after a thirteen-year waiting period, my sister was about to get kicked off our application. While my mom, dad, and I would all be able to become permanent residents, my twenty-one-year-old sister would have to start the process all over again. If that happened, her only hope would be temporarily marrying our cousin (who, unbeknownst to us at the time, happened to be gay and in a committed relationship).

Anytime my sister called from college to catch up, I had to keep the terrible aging-out secret from her. My parents insisted that we didn't mention it to Samira. Why worry her if we could manage to alleviate the issue? She was in the middle of finals and there was no way she'd be able to concentrate if she knew about what we were dealing with back home. Nearly five years before, she had been the one to break the news to me that we were at risk of getting deported, but I couldn't bring myself to tell her that she might be the illegal immigrant black sheep of the family.

In a nutshell, here's how the process worked and exactly what we were up against. We received a notice in the mail that our application for green cards (through my uncle) was being considered. It had been more than fifteen years since we'd moved to the country, so we were beside ourselves that our illegal immigration problems were finally coming to a close. But what followed was more waiting. After your application makes it to the top of the pile, you get another notice in the mail for an appointment to get your fingerprints taken, which are used for a background check. Once your background check gets approved, you receive your interview notice in the mail. The process after the "your background check is up to snuff" letter can still take years. But we didn't have the luxury of time on our side anymore. My sister *had to* get her interview date on the books before her birthday or she was screwed. So our lawyer (also known as the white savior in this story) rushed my mom's and my sister's applications. This meant once their fingerprints were received, they'd immediately get assigned an interview date and my sister would avoid aging out.

With a few days to spare, my mom and sister got their fingerprints sent in, and it seemed like everything was falling into place . . . until a storm on the East Coast threw a major wrench into the plan. Due to bad weather, it looked like the fingerprints would not arrive in DC in time. Samira was going to turn twenty-one on Monday, June 22, 1998. By Friday, June 19, there was still no indication that the fingerprints had been received and that the interview date had come through. At this point, my parents were more desperate than they'd ever been. So they decided to drive straight to the INS and beg. The offices were closed when they arrived, but they banged on the door and asked a janitor to let them in. (This was pre-9/11. I have a feeling they'd be arrested for that now.) When the janitor saw that they were both in tears, he took pity on them and ushered them inside. They must have looked pitiful enough, because they managed to get face time with the immigration officer on their case.

The officer stared back at them blankly as they explained their predicament, and then he cut them off.

"I don't know why you're here," he said. "The fingerprints were received for your daughter. Everything is fine. She has her interview date."

In an era without cell phones, our lawyer had been trying to reach my parents to let them know my sister's application was in the clear, but they were already banging on the doors of the INS. Our lawyer even called my uncle to tell him, but no one was able to reach my parents. And that's why it was the immigration officer who broke the good news. My dad was so overcome with joy and relief that he pulled the man into a bear hug. My sister was only filled in on the story after the fact, and by the summer of 1998, she and my mom finally got their green cards. To put things in perspective, it would take another *two years* for me and my dad to become permanent residents. If we hadn't been able to get a rush on my sister's application, she'd probably still be waiting to become a legal immigrant.

I remember my interview at the INS well. By then, I was going into my junior year of college at UC Berkeley. After two years of debauchery at UC Santa Cruz, my immigrant child guilt complex kicked in, and I decided I couldn't let my parents pay for a college education that included no grades, narrative evaluations, and a stump on campus that doubled as a bong. I needed something more academic, so I made the move to Cal and suffered through life as a junior transfer with no friends and no social life. My isolation was compounded by the fact that during a weekend home visiting my parents, I had the urge to get my hair cut on a Saturday without an appointment. I slipped into a salon in the posh town of Los Gatos, and every ounce of my being told me to run the other way when I was greeted by a hairstylist who was definitely in the witness protection program and hiding out from the mob. I showed him a cute photo I'd found of Kate Winslet with a layered bob. When I left his salon, I had an uneven, boy-short pixie cut. I went to a stylist in Berkeley to get the cut fixed and she looked at me and said, "This is the worst haircut I've ever seen in my life."

In order to fix his screwup, she had to trim my hair even shorter. So when I arrived at the INS with my parents for my interview, I was the spitting image of Justin Bieber. As previously mentioned, I still hadn't gotten over my sterling-silver-ring phase, and my mom was utterly horrified. Despite my questionable physical appearance, I charmed the immigration officer, answered a bunch of benign questions, and walked out knowing that I'd finally be getting a green card. The whole process took an hour, tops. Actually, the *whole* process took eighteen years, but the end felt deceptively easy.

The financial benefits of becoming a permanent resident would also finally ease the burden of college tuition on my parents. After three years of struggling to pay my tuition out of pocket, we were finally able to apply for financial aid for my senior year. The timing had worked out similarly for my sister when, two years prior, they were able to get a loan to pay for her last year of college. But getting a green card wouldn't be the ending to our story. I still wanted to become an American citizen. For years, I'd claimed to friends, classmates, and co-workers that I'd held on to my Iranian citizenship because I wanted to travel back to Tehran at some point and it would be much more difficult on a US passport. This wasn't a lie exactly, but the real reason I wasn't a citizen was that you had to have a green card for five years before you could become one. And thus becoming a permanent resident marked the beginning of our next chapter of waiting.

Five more years. Five more years and I could finally vote in an election and not get patted down at airports purely because my last name was Saedi and I had an Iranian passport. Five more years and I would officially become an *American*. On paper, anyway.

FREQUENTLY ASKED QUESTION #7
I'm undocumented and I'm scared. Any words of advice?

I was scared, too. I was scared a lot of the time. There are some details of my family's immigration story that I've chosen to leave out of this book, because I'm still scared we could get in trouble for having been here illegally for so long (especially considering the unpredictable times we're living in). For undocumented immigrants, past or present, the fear becomes a normal part of our daily lives. Even after the relief of getting a green card or becoming an American citizen, it's easy to channel my days as an "illegal alien" and feel the anxiety all over again. So I'm not being disingenuous when I say that I feel your pain.

As of now, it's impossible to know what the future holds, but we're living in a much scarier era for immigrants (and other marginalized groups) than when I was growing up. In fact, it was Republican president Ronald Reagan who granted amnesty to nearly three million undocumented immigrants in 1986. (Our family was ineligible, because anmesty was only granted to those who came to the country before 1982.) And, now, we're certainly living in a much more terrifying time than we did under the Obama presidency. Some called former president Barack Obama the deporter in chief, because his administration deported more undocumented immigrants than any president before him. This isn't totally inaccurate, but it's also likely that Obama took a hard line against immigrants with serious criminal records in hopes of passing legislation that would help undocumented families and children stay together.

In June 2012, the Obama administration implemented **Deferred Action for Childhood Arrivals (DACA)** by way of executive order. This was primarily in response to the **Development, Relief, and Education for Alien Minors (DREAM) Act's** failure to pass in Congress. Under DACA, undocumented children who entered the United States before the age of sixteen would avoid deportation. However, the executive order only bestowed temporary legal presence and work authorization. To become a permanent resident, a DACA recipient had to qualify through another basis (normally, through a spouse or a child over the age of 21 who is a US citizen.)

Then, in November 2014, also under executive action, Obama announced an immigration policy that would have helped millions of other undocumented immigrants by also giving them work permits and "deferred action" (basically, a safeguard against deportation). The new program was called **Deferred Action for Parents of Americans and Lawful Permanent Residents (DAPA)**. I spoke to my cousin Kianoush Naficy Curran, a former immigration lawyer, and she referred to DAPA as what every immigration lawyer she knew had been waiting for, because it would have helped legalize so many people who had lived and worked in the shadows for years.

Unfortunately, DAPA was halted by the court system, and when the case (*United States v. Texas*) eventually made it to the Supreme Court, which at the time had only eight members, the justices handed down a split decision. Thus, the lower appellate court's holding (that Obama did not have the right to implement the program) remained the final word, and DAPA never went into effect. This was the state of immigration reform under a leader who had progressive and humane intentions on the issue, and was stonewalled and thwarted at every turn.*

During his presidential campaign, Donald Trump talked about building walls and deporting the eleven million undocumented immigrants currently living in the United States. There are people across the country who not only championed those policies but also cited them as the reason they voted for him. On November 8, 2016, as I watched the election results with the rest of the country, I experienced waves of panic, broken up only by heavy sobs. Throughout the night, my sister and I called each other. If she was the one spiraling, I tried to calm her down. If I was the one spiraling, she tried to calm me down. As the sun came up the next day, I didn't know what to mourn first. As a female, a minority, and an immigrant, I felt lost. And I don't blame my confusion on living in a bubble. Yes, I grew up and live in one of the most liberal states in the nation. I know parts of the country relate to me about as much as I relate to

---

*Sadly, on September 5, 2017 (and as of this writing), President Trump rescinded DACA, giving Congress six months to pass legislation on immigration reform—all while putting the lives of 800,000 young people in limbo.

them, but I had mistakenly thought that even if our lives were undeniably different, we were still connected by our humanity. And that, ultimately, our morals would prevent us from electing someone who promoted racism and misogyny and xenophobia. Also, I *really* wanted to witness Hillary Clinton become the first female president.

That didn't happen, which may be why you're more afraid now than you've ever been. It's impossible for me to know how the country's policy on immigration will change, but after the fallout from an executive order to turn away refugees and ban citizens from Iran, Libya, Somalia, Sudan, Syria, and Yemen from entering the United States, the future seems even more uncertain. In June 2017, the Supreme Court upheld parts of the executive order allowing a ban on foreign nationals from those countries who have no "bona fide relationship with any person or entity in the United States." The decision was deemed a victory for the Trump administration. The court will hear the case in the fall of 2017, but as of this writing, the restrictions stand.

Despite the direction the country is headed, it's helpful to remember that you have options and you have rights. There are millions of activists who have mobilized after the election on your behalf, but you can do your part, too. A little legal advice from my cousin: as a young person without immigration status, you must avoid a criminal record at all costs. Trump has said he would focus on deporting immigrants with a record, but that could translate to a single DUI or a simple misdemeanor. If fifteen-year-old me had been caught smoking pot and these proposed policies were in place, I would have been shipped away. Luckily, places like California and New York City have said they would not aid the federal government in deporting undocumented immigrants and have created safe zones on school campuses that would prevent federal immigration officials from entering.

But there are also basic defensive strategies you yourself can employ. Despite being undocumented, you have the right to a fair hearing and a right to find an attorney (even though the government has no obligation to provide one for you). You should never sign paperwork you don't understand. Most important, never open the door for any immigration enforcement officer unless you are presented with a warrant that the officer has slipped under your door. Being afraid does not have to mean giving into intimidation tactics.

A few days after the election, I was still in a fog. I walked into the ladies' room at my office, and this is what I saw on the mirror:

I realize it's just six words on a Post-it note, but for a moment at least, it filled me with hope. I didn't know then that it was the beginning of a movement. A couple months later, I stood among hundreds of thousands of protesters at the Women's March in Los Angeles. A few days after that, I watched as protesters gathered at major airports across the country to denounce the ban on Syrian refugees and Muslims around the world. It reminded me that none of us are alone in this. Even if you feel like you have to stay hidden, there are millions who will gladly keep fighting on your behalf—myself included. All of that said, if it turns out that I've been shipped to a Muslim internment camp, please send help—and copious amounts of cheese and crackers.

I hereby declare, on oath, that I absolutely and entirely renounce and abjure all allegiance and fidelity to any foreign prince, potentate, state, or sovereignty, of whom or which I have heretofore been a subject or citizen; that I will support and defend the Constitution and laws of the United States of America against all enemies, foreign and domestic.

—Excerpt from the Naturalization Oath of Allegiance to the United States of America

Chapter Fifteen

★ ◆

I Am a Spork

The scorching temperatures in Pomona were unbearable that day. Even with my air conditioner on full blast, I could already tell that I was sweating through my wrap dress. It wasn't just the heat that was making me perspire but my nerves about what lay ahead. Right now, in my car, I was still an Iranian citizen. But in a couple of hours, that lifelong fact about me, the one that always seemed to surprise people, would no longer be true. I didn't know how I was supposed to feel. Elated? Indifferent? Obnoxiously patriotic? I periodically glanced at my printed-out MapQuest directions until I came upon the Fairplex and pulled into the massive parking lot. I was late. There was already row after row of parked cars, and I suddenly felt like I was attending a carnival and not a swearing-in ceremony.

I'm not sure what I expected, but this wasn't it. As I made the long walk from my car to the entrance of the building that normally housed the county fair, I moved past vendors selling hot dogs, American flags, and T-shirts. It was like we were being welcomed into the country by capitalism and obesity. I decided not to shell out any of my hard-earned cash on cheap memorabilia . . . though celebrating with transfat was tempting.

It was 2005, and I wasn't too keen on the American government during that period. President Bush had famously referred to Iran as part of an axis of evil, and after twenty-four years of living in the United States, I felt like the Middle East was even more misunderstood than during the hostage crisis or the Gulf War. Everyone who wasn't related to me made a huge fuss over the news that I was about to become a citizen. I received a barrage of congratulations from my work colleagues and from my American boyfriend's family. I suppose it was a big deal, but for some reason getting congratulated for becoming an American citizen brought on a slight feeling of discomfort. The reactions seemed to suggest that being an American was better than being anything else.

"You're one of us now!" I could hear people saying underneath their cheerful rhetoric.

And then I could hear my parents' voice from when I was a teenager . . .

"You're becoming *too* American."

Or maybe what they meant to say was, "You're not one of us anymore."

It wasn't like I was going to be the first in my immediate family to take the plunge and become a citizen. Kia had been one from the moment he entered the world. Maman and Samira were still two years ahead of me in the process and had already traded in their green cards for US passports. Since I'd become a permanent resident, I'd suffered through two frustrating presidential elections without being allowed to vote, and it was important to me to exercise my democratic right in the next one. But voting booths aside, I worried I'd be betraying my Iranian side if I was too gung ho about becoming fully Americanized. And so I treated the swearing-in ceremony like it was a movie with an exhaustingly slow build and an anticlimactic ending.

I raised my right hand as directed and looked around nervously at the other hundreds of participants while a video of an imposing President Bush stared down at us like Big Brother. The acoustics in the Fairplex were so poor that none of us could understand a word of what the president was saying. We were supposed to repeat the words of the naturalization oath as he said them, but his voice echoed off the walls incoherently. A roomful of immigrants smiled and shrugged at each other as we all made a lame attempt to follow along. On the sidelines, family members waved flags and hollered. I wondered if I should have brought along my boyfriend to make the experience feel more real or important, but I hadn't expected it to be a spectator sport. Instead, I did the most *American* thing I could have done during the rest of the ceremony: I worked. For the last few years, I'd been employed as a creative executive at ABC Daytime, and I'd gotten adept at finding windows of opportunity to catch up on scripts. While everyone else grinned from ear to ear with the promise of the future, I flipped through the pages of an episode of *General Hospital*.

Looking back, I regret my behavior. I wish I had left the script in the car. What did other people think as they looked at me, keeping my head buried in an episode of a television show? It probably seemed like I was belittling a moment they'd been waiting years to experience. Perhaps they assumed my path to citizenship was painless, smooth, and easy. If it had been arduous and traumatic, then I'd be savoring every second of the occasion. I finally put down the script when it came time to announce every country that was represented in the room. As cheers rippled through the crowd, it felt like we'd all gathered at the World Cup. I yelled loudly when Iran was announced. In that moment, being surrounded by a diverse group of ethnicities—all of us about to become citizens together—I realized that *this* is what I loved about America. *This* was why I was proud to be here. I was about to become part of a country that was much more rich and interesting because it had no walls built around its perimeter.

By the end of the ceremony, I was far less cynical about the whole event. This was the true end of our immigration nightmare. I was two when we moved to the United States, and at the age of twenty-six, I was finally an American citizen. After the ceremony ended, we were directed to wait in a line that corresponded with our last name to turn over our green card and to receive a certificate of naturalization.

Once I received my certificate, I hurried through the parking lot to get back to work, but it took nearly an hour to find my car among the massive and indistinguishable rows of vehicles. Later that week, my co-workers surprised me with cake and a congratulatory card, and I thanked them and allowed myself to recognize the significance of the experience.

The proud moments have continued since. Like the weekend in 2008 when my cousins and I piled into a twelve-passenger van in Los Angeles and drove the four hours to Las Vegas to canvass for the candidate who would become our first black president. Or casting a vote for the first female presidential candidate of a major party. I've learned not to take democracy or my vote for granted, especially having seen how elections brought on tumultuous times in Iran. But that doesn't mean I'm not constantly balancing my American-ness with my Iranian-ness. I've walked that line long enough to know it's a balance I'll never perfect or maintain. I can keep attempting it, but I'll always seem too Iranian for some and too American for others. I try to ignore the raised eyebrows when I say I want my child to learn to speak Farsi despite my loosening grasp on the language. I try to politely bite my tongue when people say, "Stop saying you're Iranian. You're an American."

My parents have accepted the amount their kids have become "Americanized." They've now lived in the States longer than they lived in Iran. Years ago, my mom made a trip back to Tehran and realized it was nothing like the country she remembered. She returned to the United States feeling like there was nowhere she truly belonged, but that doesn't mean she and my dad don't still mourn the loss of another one of our Iranian habits.

"You eat rice with a fork now?" my baba asked a few years ago as he watched me eat my dinner.

It was an innocent question, but I could sense the disappointment in his tone. I'd lived with my American boyfriend-turned-husband for more than five years by then. We rarely even ate rice, but when we did, I'd grown accustomed to using a fork, the same way he did, even though the utensil never made sense to me in that context. Tiny grains of rice would inevitably fall through the prongs of the fork. "Why am I not using a spoon?" I'd wonder.

After my dad pointed out my poor utensil choice, the guilt got to me and I went back to using a spoon. It took a while to get reacquainted with my old habit, but while I scooped up my rice with a spoon, it dawned on me: I am a spork.

I'm the combination of two worlds and cultures. I may not be the most traditional or obvious choice. There may not be a built-in slot for me in a standard utensil tray, but it doesn't matter. I don't need to fit into a compartment to be proud of where I've come from (however illegally) and where I am now.

An Open Letter to Myself

Dear Sara who never left Iran,

Even though you don't technically exist, I've thought a lot about you. What if my parents had decided to wait out the revolution and the war? What if they hadn't had the guts to leave Iran and try to give us a better life in America? What if we got deported and I spent most of my adolescence back in Tehran? I've wondered how we'd be the same and how we'd be different. I imagine you're still witty and sassy, and that your Farsi puts mine to shame. Maybe you even gave in to societal pressures and got a nose job. Or maybe you were far less self-conscious of your looks than I was growing up, since you lived in a country that puts far less emphasis on sexualizing women. I also bet you've written more books than me just with the hours you saved throwing on a head scarf to disguise a bad hair day instead of spending a ridiculous amount of time blowing out your curly, unmanageable locks.

Or maybe you didn't feel as compelled to have a career or follow your passions in Iran. Perhaps our priorities would have been completely different. When I was busy applying for colleges, you may have been weighing the pros and cons of going to university versus getting married right away. Instead of considering undergraduate programs, you may have been considering potential suitors. I have a feeling your journal entries were more introspective and philosophical. Hopefully, you didn't fill most of the pages lamenting the fact that the boy you loved didn't love you back. I wonder if you secretly had boyfriends throughout the years, or if you went straight from living with Maman and Baba to getting married. I hope you had an opportunity to live on your own first, but it's quite possible you'd be the mother to teenagers by now.

Are you content living in Iran? Do you walk the streets of Tehran and marvel at the architecture and haggle your way through crowded bazaars? Or do you go to sleep wondering about me? Do you think about what your life would have been like if you'd gotten to live in America? You've probably seen more of the world than I have. I wasn't allowed to travel out of the country until I was twenty, but I bet Maman and Baba took you on family vacations to places like Barcelona and Paris and Florence . . . if those countries granted you a visitor's visa.

Do you know how to cook all of my favorite Persian dishes? I always complained about eating Iranian food growing up, and now I'd do anything to eat it at every meal. I didn't take an interest in learning how to properly make tahdig (ridiculously delicious crispy rice). But I bet your Persian husband and children praise your culinary skills.

I wonder where you were during the Green Movement in 2009.* Did you stay indoors where it was safe, or did you take to the streets with the other protesters? Did you chant "Where is my vote?" till you were hoarse? Do you know anyone who was killed? I'll tell you where I was on the day of the fateful election. I drove to a hotel in West Los Angeles to vote for your president. With my Iranian passport handy, I was allowed to cast a vote in a country I hadn't lived in since I was two years old. The result of the election may not have impacted my life at all, or if it turned Iran into a more progressive country, it might have made it less difficult to travel to places like Tehran and Shiraz and Isfahan.

I practiced the night before how to write the candidate's name in Farsi. You may be shocked to hear this, but my Farsi is at a first-grade reading and writing level. I'm essentially illiterate in my native language. After I finished voting, I returned to my car and got stuck at a red light next to a rowdy group of Iranian protesters and shah supporters. One of them was frantically yelling at me to roll down my window. I thought she merely wanted to warn me that I had a flat tire. I

*The Green Movement was a political uprising in Iran that was ignited by the 2009 election. Supporters of the more progressive candidate, Mir Hossein Moussavi, took to the streets after what they felt was a rigged election. They fought for the removal of President Ahmadinejad. The Iranian government reported that thirty-six people died in the protests, but the opposition party alleged that more than twice that number were killed. The movement was also dubbed the Twitter Revolution, because protesters used the social networking site to mobilize and communicate with each other. Ultimately, Ahmadinejad was sworn in for a second term, but the Green Movement exposed corruption—and dissension—within the regime. It also became a lasting symbol of unity and hope.

made the mistake of rolling my window down, and she started screaming at me in Farsi. She said that voting in the election meant supporting a regime that sent young girls to be sex slaves in Dubai. I had no idea about sex slaves in Dubai. And even if I did, I didn't know how to debate her in Farsi. I was speechless.

So I stared at the woman blankly, and in perfect English, I said: "I'm so sorry, but I have no idea what you're saying."

"You didn't vote in the election?" the woman asked me, confused.

"What election?" I replied.

The light changed from red to green, and I could hear her fellow protesters teasing her for mistaking me for an Iranian.

"I don't know," I heard the woman say in Farsi. "She sort of looked like she could be Iranian."

While your country was in a political crisis and young people were getting shot at by the police, I was essentially passing for white. For about a week, I was glued to the news and wore a green wristband in solidarity. The Green Movement eventually dissipated, and I stopped thinking about you and went on with my relatively easy existence. I concerned myself with career changes and the adjustment period of living with a boyfriend for the first time. I voted in elections that didn't end in protests. I voted in elections that did. I thought of you and the youth of Iran while marching the streets of my own city, chanting "This is democracy." I mourned the loss of my grandma, and wondered if I'd ever be able to travel to Iran to visit her grave. Maybe while strolling through the sidewalks of the Jordan district that she loved to visit, I would meet a woman like you. Over tea, we'd compare notes and be unsurprised by all the ways we are different. But hopefully, we'd also stumble upon the ways we are the same: the love for our family, the pride in our culture, the frustrations with our culture, and how we both agreed that cooking ghormeh sabzi* from scratch takes way too damn long. We would realize that finding common ground does not require living in the same country or even the same part of the world, and that despite our vastly different upbringings, there's so much more that connects us than separates us. And then maybe you'd be able to convince me to get my nose done.

Love,
The Americanized Sara

---

*An herb stew and one of the most popular Persian dishes. It's often considered the national dish of Iran. It's out of this world, but preparing it is very labor-intensive.

YOUR UNDOCUMENTED IMMIGRANT
REFRESHER COURSE!

At this point in the book, you are hopefully more knowledgeable about our country's immigration policies. But just in case you're still fuzzy on the details, here's a handy refresher. Think of it as "Undocumented Immigration for Dummies." There are hundreds of different immigration scenarios, but I'll focus on the path my family took to get naturalized.

First, we moved to America on a **visitor's visa** to escape Iran. A visitor's visa grants you entry into the country for a temporary period of time. When that visa expired, we filed for **political asylum.** This is a route you take to become a legal resident of the United States when you're escaping persecution in your home country, and when returning to said country could put your life at risk. Many Iranians who fled the country during the revolution were granted political asylum.* The downside of getting political asylum is that returning to your homeland (even for a visit) could make it impossible to return to the United States, which means that most people who are granted asylum never go back to their country. But this route didn't work out for my family because, after waiting for two years, we were informed that there was no record of our application.

---

*An "asylee" is different than a "refugee." Refugee status can only be granted to someone who is outside of the US. An asylum seeker must already be present in the US.

It was then that we decided to apply for **adjustment of status.** This is what you do when you're living in the United States with some form of temporary status (we were able to take this route since we entered the country on a visitor's visa). It also allows you to apply for a green card without returning abroad. But for those who crossed the border without inspection, adjusting status is almost impossible due to their illegal entry. We were very lucky on that front. Those of us with temporary status also have a variety of methods to apply for adjustment of status. For instance, you can marry someone who's an American citizen and receive a green card through your spouse. This is the fastest route and doesn't come with any of the long waiting periods. You can also be sponsored through an employer if you can prove that no one else can do your particular job. If you're wealthy and can afford to do $500,000 or more in business in the United States, you can also be granted a green card. This particular application is called an EB-5. Some equate it to buying your way into becoming a permanent resident. Others argue that a person who's going to put money into the American economy should be given priority for legal residency.

If none of these methods are applicable, you can be sponsored through a family member who is either an American citizen or a permanent resident. This route comes with an incredibly long waiting period, but it's the only course of action my family was able to take. We filed two applications—one through my uncle, and one through my grandmother. When my grandmother passed away, that application became null and void. The application with my uncle took fifteen years to be approved. In fact, filing through a sibling is one of the slowest ways to become a legal resident. Why? Well, there are quotas, which means only a certain number of applications are approved each year in each category. The sibling category has one of the smaller quotas, which leads to the long wait times. You can look up the visa bulletin website for current wait times for each category. As I write this, applicants from 2003 are finally getting green cards through the sibling route. It's even worse for citizens from the Philippines and Mexico, where applicants from 1994 and 1997, respectively, are up for consideration. On average, the United States approves one million applicants annually as permanent residents. According to **US Citizenship and Immigration Services (USCIS),** they receive six million applications a year from employers and individuals—either to permanently live in the country, temporarily work in the country, or become a citizen.

When it comes to the debate surrounding immigration reform, some argue that the breakdown of quotas needs to be changed. For instance, should more green cards be awarded through employers? If someone is an engineer and is going to contribute to innovation in the United States, then shouldn't they have priority over someone who simply has a family member who lives in the country? Or is there a moral responsibility to keep families together that takes precedence over quotas that focus on career endeavors (especially since separating young children from their parents could open a costly can of worms)? Every country has a different philosophy on the topic. Consider the fact that Canada has taken in twenty-five thousand Syrian refugees, while Obama's plan to bring in ten thousand refugees was met with outrage in Congress. And as of this writing, Trump has placed a ban on all Syrian refugees.

It's important to remember that once your adjustment-of-status application is pending, you will not be subjected to random deportation unless you commit a crime. The pending period is sort of like a safe zone, but the fear and anxiety lie in your application getting denied. If that happens, then the government has every right to force you to leave the country.

Also, if you don't already have an employment authorization card or a Social Security number, you can obtain both as part of your adjustment-of-status application. When we filed an application through my uncle, my sister and I were finally issued work permits, which we were able to use to obtain our own Social Security numbers. It's also important to remember that undocumented immigrants with work permits and Social Security numbers do in fact pay taxes. I was a pro at filling out a 1040EZ back when I got paid chump change at Baskin-Robbins.

Once your application is finally being considered, you receive a notice to get your fingerprints taken. The USCIS has their own authorized fingerprint sites, and they give you a specific date and time to have your prints taken. After your fingerprints are submitted, the FBI conducts a thorough background check. Once the background check proves you've been on the up and up, then you're issued an interview date at USCIS. This feels like winning the lottery for anyone who's been waiting a long time to get a green card. The interview is rather straightforward, but probably much more nerve-racking for non–English speakers. If all goes well, then you finally become a legal resident of the United States. Huzzah!

My sister nearly **"aged out"** of our adjustment-of-status application when she was on the brink of turning twenty-one before our application was approved. This was in 1998. But in 2002, the **Child Status Protection Act (CSPA)** was passed. Congress recognized that many children on applications were aging out, due to extremely long processing times for applications. Thanks to the CSPA, a beneficiary can retain "child" status even if they've reached age twenty-one. But here's the catch. The petition for a green card has to be filed through an immediate family member, and the "child" has to remain unmarried. So even if the CSPA had been in effect in the nineties, it wouldn't have protected my sister, since we filed through my uncle, who's not considered an immediate family member.

Once you receive your green card, you have to wait five years before you can apply to become an American citizen. What follows is another series of fingerprints and an interview that requires a ten-question civics test (chosen from a possible one hundred questions). If you pass the test and the interview, you'll receive a notice for your swearing-in ceremony. After a lot of flag waving and oath taking, you'll officially become an American citizen. You may feel a sense of pride or relief as you receive your citizenship certificate, but my hope is that you'll hold on to the memories of what life was like before you were a permanent resident or a United States citizen so that you can spread empathy for those who are still struggling to legally belong here.

Acknowledgments

My high school diaries.

This book would not have been possible without the hard work of so many. Luckily, there's no orchestra to play me off in the middle of this:

Thank you to Jess Regel at Foundry Literary & Media for refusing to take no for an answer and telling me to write my story. You were on this journey with me from day one and I thank my lucky stars every day that I found you.

None of this would have happened without my amazing editor, Kelly Delaney at Knopf. I can't thank you enough for shepherding this project. You never steered me wrong. Your passion and empathy are unmatched, and I'm so grateful for your spot-on notes, suggestions, and contributions.

There were so many other wonderful people at Knopf who helped make this book a reality.

Thank you to Alison Impey for your beautiful cover design. If sixteen-year-old me could have seen it, she would have felt a lot cooler in high school. Thank you to Trish Parcell for bringing a boring Word document to life with your inspired interior design—and for solving our diary entry conundrum. Thank you to Erica Ferguson for your very thorough, and oftentimes hilarious, copyedits. We may have been separated at birth. Thank you as well to Janet Renard, Amy Schroeder, and Artie Bennett for your copyedits and for catching all the embarrassing typos. I hope you kept in mind that English is my second language. And thank you to William Adams for the legal guidance. Thank you to the book's managing editor, Dawn Ryan, for your tireless work. Mabel + Rocky forever. And last, thank you to Alexandra Gottlieb for your enthusiasm and kind words about this project. It meant so much to me.

To Lynn Fimberg, David Rubin, Eric Brooks, Michael Pelmont, and Matt Ochacher for the frequent pep talks and unwavering support.

Thank you to Susan Levine and Jane Reardon for your continued advice and confidence boosts.

To my dear friends Aleka Seville and Megan Carroll for making my teen years so much more bearable (and memorable).

Nastaran Dibai—you're one of my writing heroes. Thank you for taking an interest in the book and encouraging me throughout.

A name check to my (first) cousins who made life as an immigrant far less lonely: Ali, Amir, Anoosheh, Arjang, Ashkan, Atefeh, Gita, Hootan, Kaveh, Kian, Ladan, Leyla, Maryam, Mehdi, Mitra, Nasiem, Neda, Omid, and Payam. A special thank-you to Omid Sanjideh, Ali Reza, and Atefeh for their expertise on all things Iran.

A huge thank-you to my (second) cousin Kianoush Naficy Curran for guiding me through immigration law and for being the best consultant a girl could ask for. I could not have done this without you.

To my khaleh Mandana, Shahrzad, and Mehrzad; my aunt Geneva; my ameh Fafar; and my dayee Mehrdad and Shahrdad for allowing me to reveal events from your past—however painful or personal. A very special thank-you to my dayee Mehrdad for reading an early draft of this book and giving such helpful feedback. Mostly, thank you for your wisdom and selflessness.

To my brother from another mother, Jake Abrams. I may have gotten an older brother later in life, but I got the best one.

This narrative is as much my sister and brother's as it is mine. Samira and Kia, thank you for trusting me with our family history and our shared adolescent experiences. The best part of writing this book was remembering how much we meant to each other as kids, and knowing how much we still mean to each other as adults. I love you both so much.

I don't even know how to properly thank my parents, Ali and Shohreh Saedi. This book is a product of every sacrifice you've made for me. If that wasn't enough, you were also my researchers, fact-checkers, and story consultants all in one. Thank you for the hours you spent answering my questions and for sharing details of your lives I'd never known. You're what every parent should be. I love you.

A lifetime of thank-yous to my husband, Bryon Schafer. I knew you were the guy for me when you were able to remember all of my cousins' names *and* tell them apart. Thank you for always believing in me and for embracing our crazy culture. I love you more than Persians love koobideh.

To my son, Ellis Ata Schafer—I was pregnant with you while writing this book, which made the experience all the more significant. I know that when you're old enough to read this, you'll be so proud of where you came from. To think—if there'd been a travel ban, you may have never existed. I love you, *pesaram*.